Fresh Air and Fun

A Blackpool Miscellany

Published by
Landy Publishing
"Acorns", 3 Staining Rise
Staining, Blackpool
Telephone: 886103

ISBN 0 9507692 3 1

Phototypeset, printed and bound by
Galava Printing Company Limited, Nelson, Lancs.

Fresh Air and Fun
(A Blackpool Miscellany)

Edited by Bob Dobson and Doreen Brotherton

Landy Publishing
1988

Foreword

"There's a famous seaside place called Blackpool,
Which is noted for fresh air and fun".

So says the immortal Stanley Holloway at the beginning of that magnificent monologue *Albert and the Lion* written by Marriot Edgar. This book is intended to let the world know that Blackpool is noted for fresh air, fun—and much more. It is, yet it isn't, a history book. It does tell of Blackpool's past but there's much more to it than just the dryness of some history books. It is a hot-pot, a miscellaneous mixture of many stories about the Blackpool of yesteryear. Some of the stories have been told before, and some haven't. We think that all the stories ought to be told, and these, the snippets and the pictures will give pleasure to Blackpool-lovers.

We dedicate this book to the memory of two people who died before the book came to life, although they had something to do with passing on to us, and many more, something of their love for Blackpool—**Kathleen Eyre** and **Arthur Murphy.**
May they be paddling and bathed in sunshine in that other heaven.

Bob Dobson and Doreen Brotherton

4

Contents

ABOUT OUR ADVERTISERS

When seeking Blackpool companies to advertise in this book, we made it clear that we wanted business from those with a strong feeling for the town. Although few responded to our call, the trio who did have strong ties indeed with Blackpool, and we feel we should tell our readers about them.

John Marsh set up his haulage firm in Dalton Street, off Abbey Road in the 1930's with one lorry. He worked on carrying soil and sand for the Corporation and private firms locally. By 1958 he had 5 tipper lorries, and started another company, Blackpool Van Transport, to expand his business. He moved to the present garage and yard on Midgeland Road about 1948. Initially, Blackpool Van Transport - known as B.V.T. - had one vehicle to its name, and up to 1964 the business was largely in carting soil and sand excavation material. Their vehicles were to be used on major Blackpool projects, such as when The Palace Theatre was knocked down for the building of Lewis' store, and bringing sand from the beach to lay on the floor of the soggy Royal Lancashire Showground near Stanley Park, and the demolition of Central Station.

Peter Haworth joined John Marsh as a fitter in 1950, and is now the General Manager and Director along with John Marsh's daughters. A Blackpool lad through and through, Peter is to be found each day (and throughout many nights) in the garage in his overalls, preparing for the road the 28 wagons in their red and white livery which are a familiar sight on motorways throughout the country, bringing the name of Blackpool to the rest of the country.

★   ★   ★   ★   ★

In the 1950's, Don Sidebottom was a student of architecture at Blackpool Technical College, and sold car stickers to keep himself in funds. His personal drive was such that he had them made to his own design before pedalling round local gift shops to sell them, and in 1959 he set up in business as Glasdon Laminates (later changed to Glasdon Signs and later still to Glasdon Limited). The Glas part of the name is from the Glass-fibre material used in products, and the Don part is from Don's name. The 250 local people Don employs feel a great deal of pride that their company is the leading manufacturer in the world of Glass Reinforced Plastic building systems, and a European leader in well-designed snow control, road safety, and litter collection equipment. Glasdon's employees are proud of their Blackpool products being seen around the world. It is a pride which starts at the desk of Don Sidebottom, who is as Blackpool as a stick of rock.

★   ★   ★   ★   ★

The Pleasure Beach has been a part of the Blackpool scene for so long that it has become an institution, famed far and wide amongst those seeking and remembering pleasure. We have an essay on the place (one tends to forget it is a company) in the book because we decided at the outset that their's was a tale that ought to be told. However, it doesn't tell of the strength of the love of Blackpool shared by it principals, Mrs Doris Thompson (Chairman) and her son Geoffrey (Managing Director), descendants of William George Bean, the founder. It doesn't tell either of the strength of the inseparable bond that makes The Pleasure Beach such an important part of Blackpool's tourist industry. To bring the story right up to date, it ought to mention that in 1987, British Rail opened a new railway station right at the door of the Pleasure Beach. That has the feel of a piece of arranging worthy of the fathers of Blackpool's pleasure business.

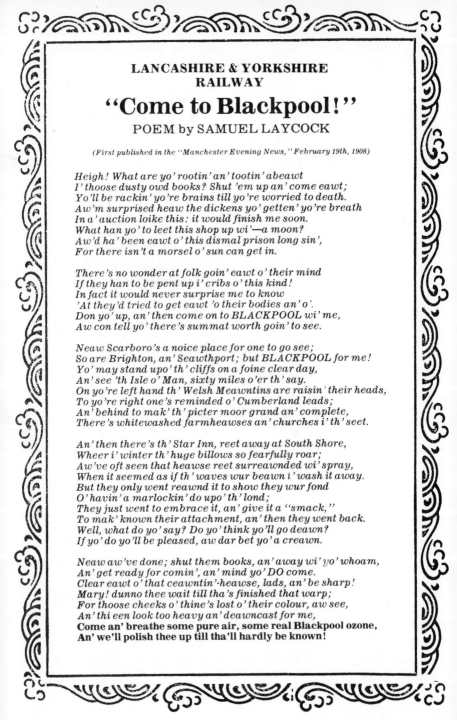

LANCASHIRE & YORKSHIRE RAILWAY

"Come to Blackpool!"

POEM by SAMUEL LAYCOCK

(First published in the "Manchester Evening News," February 19th, 1908)

Heigh! What are yo' rootin' an' tootin' abeawt
I' thoose dusty owd books? Shut 'em up an' come eawt;
Yo'll be rackin' yo're brains till yo're worried to death.
Aw'm surprised heaw the dickens yo' getten' yo're breath
In a' auction loike this: it would finish me soon.
What han yo' to leet this shop up wi'—a moon?
Aw'd ha' been eawt o' this dismal prison long sin',
For there isn't a morsel o' sun can get in.

There's no wonder at folk goin' eawt o' their mind
If they han to be pent up i' cribs o' this kind!
In fact it would never surprise me to know
'At they'd tried to get eawt 'o their bodies an' o'.
Don yo' up, an' then come on to BLACKPOOL wi' me,
Aw con tell yo' there's summat worth goin' to see.

Neaw Scarboro's a noice place for one to go see;
So are Brighton, an' Seawthport; but BLACKPOOL for me!
Yo' may stand upo' th' cliffs on a foine clear day,
An' see 'th Isle o' Man, sixty miles o'er th' say.
On yo're left hand th' Welsh Meawntins are raisin' their heads,
To yo're right one's reminded o' Cumberland leads;
An' behind to mak' th' picter moor grand an' complete,
There's whitewashed farmheawses an' churches i' th' seet.

An' then there's th' Star Inn, reet away at South Shore,
Wheer i' winter th' huge billows so fearfully roar;
Aw've oft seen that heawse reet surreawnded wi' spray,
When it seemed as if th' waves wur beawn i' wash it away.
But they only went reawnd it to show they wur fond
O' havin' a marlockin' do upo' th' lond;
They just went to embrace it, an' give it a "smack,"
To mak' known their attachment, an' then they went back.
Well, what do yo' say? Do yo' think yo'll go deawn?
If yo' do yo'll be pleased, aw dar bet yo' a creawn.

Neaw aw've done; shut them books, an' away wi' yo' whoam,
An' get ready for comin', an' mind yo' DO come.
Clear eawt o' that ceawntin'-heawse, lads, an' be sharp!
Mary! dunno thee wait till tha's finished that warp;
For thoose cheeks o' thine's lost o' their colour, aw see,
An' thi een look too heavy an' deawncast for me,
Come an' breathe some pure air, some real Blackpool ozone,
An' we'll polish thee up till tha'll hardly be known!

BLACKPOOL REMEMBERED   by Reg Baxter

Characters have emerged from the Blackpool people as
from any other town's population. One of the most notable
was a co-founder of the Blackpool Tower Company—Sir
John Bickerstaffe. Ruddy-faced, with a peaked sailor's
cap (in summer this had a white top), and wearing a
white "imperial beard", he could be seen from a long way
off and could also be feared by the more timid or lazy
employees of his massive entertainment company. He
himself was of real pioneer stock, and the making of
Blackpool as a resort was the second of his ambitions; the
first one being money-making. He loved money, and he
adored rainy weather—because it sent the tens of
thousands of visitors into the precincts of t'Tower and
filled its (and his) coffers. The story was that each night
before he went to bed he would phone the Secretary's office
of the Tower Co., to be advised of what that day's takings
were.

Another personality was a voluble, black-mustachioed,
flat-capped, quick-walking, bus-riding passenger called
"Sep" (Septimus) Smith. He was a gipsy and came from
the famous Gipsy Smith stock. A dealer in everything
and anything, he was a builder of sorts, and erected
modest houses in the Marton and Ansdell Road areas of
the town. Almost all his very quick, stacato conversation
(he never welcomed comments from a listener unless they
were in agreement or flattering)—revolved around local
politics, mostly very critical of all the then Councillors.
It was invariably in rhyme, like Gilbert's lyrics to
Sullivan's music, and he **never** had to hesitate even for
one word,—like a machine-gun. He had some telling,
true, radical, and acid comments, and would hold a bus
full of listeners fascinated by his speeches. He **never** wore
a top coat. His only really famous platform as a would-be
Councillor (he was never elected) was the obvious
unfairness of females having to pay for the use of public
lavatories; and he would go on at great length, comparing
this imposition with the Middle Ages and Roman times,

9

when such payment was never demanded. He built a string of houses near Waterloo Road and named the avenue "SEP AVENUE"; but the local authority would not allow this and re-named it, with their road name sign, "DOVER ROAD". For many months Sep had nailed underneath this sign one of his own which read "This is Sep Avenue, always has been, and always will be". It is still Dover Road.

A third character was one Eli Percival who was a collector of fine things, of bric-a-brac, of garden ornaments, etc. He was a tiny, cheery-faced man,—again with a sailor cap, and his big house at the top of Adelaide Street, the corner of Leopold Grove it seemed to be, had a garden absolutely chock-full of figurines, plant stands, marble ornaments, sundials, stone statuettes, iron chairs, filigree seats, hanging baskets, etc.,—a really good free show. And the fact is that, in those days, nothing was ever illegally removed—no vandalism,—the stuff was there day and night, unattended, safe.

Most people have heard of Pablo. Ice-cream is an Italian speciality—or was. It would be overstating the case to say Mr Pablo brought ice-cream to Blackpool—but he certainly popularised it by such an extent as to produce the same effect. He was a well-marked personality if only because of his appearance....tanned with a black handle-bar moustache....usually in cream coloured garb —jacket and pants—with a white trilby, riding about in an open black Ford car which had its steering-wheel in the centre of the front bench seat not on the right, as now. Actually, Mr Pablo was a communist-thinking chap; he was a street-sweeper to start with and he helped form the first trade union in this town. His business was built up because of his generous portions of most excellent ice-cream which he had served in a sort-of parlour up some stairs at the back of Charnley Road. Kindness oozed out of him; his staff were treated to a holiday abroad at the end of each summer; and, at the end of the season, he devoted a Saturday to free ice-cream for all the children who would call at his parlour. Reticent, in that he would not push himself or his views or his business even— nevertheless he made Blackpool a more popular resort, as almost all visitors looked forward to tasting his products. He sold his business to a consortium, but the name Pablo is still in use.

There used to be a haberdashery and materials-selling place in Church Street, almost opposite Coronation Street—a kind of open little market. It was called

Whewells. The lady there will always stick in my memory. She was fat, very fat. So fat that I never once saw her leave her big wooden chair. This would be about 1923/4/5. She used tongs made out of wood to grasp hold of any article one wished to buy from her—extending tongs which could reach as far as tens of feet. And she had a cup on a rod to take money from each customer.

Another memorable sales spot was the open-fronted building (one of many) where C. & A. is now. In the twenties this was the forerunner of, first, Feldman's Theatre which later became the Queens Theatre. It was devoted to the sale of sheet music. There was a staff of about five; a pianist, a guy who led us all, kids and adults, in singing the music; another fellow to turn over the pages of a massive "book" which was suspended from a stand and which pages were flicked over the top like modern calendars, and which contained in large lettering all the words of each song as it was skilfully "demonstrated". Then the remaining staff would sell the sheet music and gee us all up for the next song. It says much for the musical skill of thousands of visitors that they were constantly buying these sheets of music so as the purveyors of it, Feldmans, Lawrence Wright, etc., made big business. I am sure that some kids who took solo parts in these demonstration spots later made quite good artists on the stage. How simple, unsophisticated, and happy, were the tastes of those days.

There are lots to remember:- Railway sleepers comprising the only walks there were round the first Pleasure Beach. The Water Chute, which, before the Big Dipper, was the greatest thrill on that amusement park. The Rainbow Wheel on the same Beach. The Bathing Machines, like tiny houses on wheels, drawn by a horse, which were trailed down onto the sands, to be occupied by undressing/dressing bathers, whose "bathing costumes" came down to their knees invariably.

Then there was Lobby Lud who strolled along the promenade carrying a Daily Mail. If you had a Daily Mail and challenged this guy by saying, "You are Lobby Lud and I claim the £5 prize", and if your Daily Mail was dated for that day, then he would hand you the prize—and what's more, your name would be in next day's paper! Fame!

The Great Wheel stood where Olympia now is. One had to stand on a platform, when it was working, and await the car coming into this little station. The arc was so gradual that one didn't realise we were climbing up until one noticed Coronation Street slowly pulling away, downwards. Each car was quite a size. They were dotted all over the Fylde for years afterwards, being used as hen houses.

I recollect the Winter Gardens Company before it merged with the Tower Company, and when it was such a "personal" company that one of the Directors had a special door built for the exclusive use of his wife and her friends and this was always known as "Mrs Ash's door".

Another feature in those days was a diver who, after being set alight and surrounded by gleaming flames, would splash into the sea from a great height at the end of the Central Pier, upon which, also, there was outdoor ballroom dancing, included in the admission charge of three (old) pence.

The open Toast Rack tramcars were another attraction, and for six old pence (a shade over 2p) one could ride from Talbot Square, up Church Street, along Whitegate Drive, down Waterloo Road, along Lytham Road, down Station Road, and along the Prom. back to Talbot Square. "The Circular" it was called.

A previously unpublished photograph, taken at the turn of the century by John Walker, a Lancaster amateur photographer. He found the sands bustling with activity, yet the grown-ups had their jackets on. There was a Punch and Judy tent, ice cream stalls and a horse-drawn cart with large wheels to take people into the water where they transferred to a sailing boat. The beach is still a marvellous place for a photographer. In this photo, the Royal Hotel is between the Tower buildings and the Palatine Hotel with its conical roof.

CATTERALL & SWARBRICKS BREWERY
by Alex Maitland

A century ago saw the beginnings of what was later to become one of the Fylde's most well-known companies. This company is no longer in existence, but will always be in the minds of many locals and holidaymakers. There are still traces of the initials 'C & S' to be found in the area on many licensed houses.

C & S was established in Poulton-le-Fylde in 1880. In Barrett's Directory for 1885 its address was giveh as Queen's Brewery, Queens Square, Poulton. In 1889 this directory also listed Richardson's Newton Springs Brewery. This was taken over by C & S in 1890 and re-named Queen's Brewery. The buildings are still there on the right hand side of Staining Road going from Normoss Road to Newton Country Club. The buildings are now used by Blackpool Tower Co. and Palatine Food Services.

On Friday, 6th July, 1894, the 'Blackpool Gazette News' said a limited liability company was to be formed of Messrs Catterall & Swarbricks Brewery.

On Saturday, 7th July, 1894, the 'Preston Guardian' carried the prospectus of the proposed new company. Its share capital was to be £50,000, comprised of 10,000 shares of £5 each. Among its directors were to be William Catterall of Breck Road, Poulton; John Swarbrick of Tower Lodge, Poulton and Tom Lockwood of The Golden Ball Hotel, Poulton.

The new company's objects were 'to acquire, extend and work the old established brewery business of Messrs. Catterall and Swarbrick'. The properties included the freehold brewery (now known as Queen's Brewery) plant, cellars (to hold up to 1000 barrels), outbuildings for bottling minerals, ales and stouts, stable for horses, hay lofts, offices and the like. The brewery had a well of excellent spring water, but the Fylde Waterworks had also laid on a mains supply in case of necessity.

Among the licensed houses were the Star Inn at Blackpool, the Saddle at Marton, three beer houses at Fleetwood, the White Bull at Great Eccleston, the Pack Horse Inn, Stalmine, the Sportsmans Arms, Poulton and the Bay Horse Hotel, Church Street, Poulton.

The new company progressed and purchased more pubs and hotels, amongst them the Victoria Hotel in Victoria Street, Blackpool for £4050 in 1896 and also in the same year, the Brewers Arms, Cocker Street, Blackpool for £7100. The business continued to flourish. New outlets were purchased or opened. An additional bottling store was built in Kent Road, Blackpool (now the home of the Central Working Men's Club). In the 1920's it was necesary for a new brewery to be built as the old one could no longer cope. A brand new modern brewery was built in Blackpool on Talbot Road, near the junction with Devonshire Road and was opened in November, 1927.

The Company's operations eventually stretched from Merseyside to the Lake District.

In 1930 C & S opened the XL Hotel on the A6 near Garstang. It was named after their XL Ales. It's name was changed in the 1960's to the Chequered Flag.

About this time the Company was using the Windmill on Preston New Road, Blackpool (now near the M.55 junction) as a store and it had *C & S XL Ales* painted on the sides in large letters.

Another popular ale was C & S Double A (Amber Ale) and was brewed until the 1940's until the company began to handle Double Diamond.

After the close of the Second World War trade began to improve and in the 1950's many of the smaller companies were taken over by the bigger ones. This became the fate of C & S in 1961 when they became part of the United Breweries Group, which in turn became part of the Charrington organisation. This merged with Bass in the late 1960's.

C & S products were gradually phased out and the parent company's lines introduced. Brewing finally ceased early in 1974. Following this, the buildings took on a new lease of life, as a warehouse, distribution centre and office H.Q. for Bass operations in the North West, serving over 350 public houses as well as free trade customers.

No doubt countless people now wish C & S could have resisted the take-over and continued to flourish in this day and age when 'real ale' as formerly brewed by C & S is so highly cherished.

C & S is dead, but not forgotten.

BLACKPOOL'S V.C.'S — by John Dullenty

When the trumpets blared and the flags flew in that malevolently naive summer of 1914 the young men of Blackpool responded to their country's call as vigorously as anywhere in the land.

And the experiences of the men who joined up spread across every facet—from digging ditches in Catterick to the terror of a Western Front bombardment, sorting service mail at Southampton to the claustrophobic anxiety of working in the magazine of a battleship at Jutland. Men signed on the dotted line and their life became a lottery. Most were just ordinary men doing ordinary work. Others, however, reached heights of bravery that few were to ascend. One such man was Second Lieutenant Alfred Victor Smith who in 1915 posthumously was awarded the Victoria Cross. He was one of the large force of Britons, Anzacs and Frenchmen who vainly bid to blast a backdoor entry into the Central Powers lair. He was 23 at the time, a Blackpool policeman and son of the Chief Constable of Burnley.

He joined the 1st/5th Battalion the East Lancashire Regiment and they were shipped to Gallipoli where the fight against the stubborn Turks was bitter and bloody. Late in December at Fusilier Bluff he was taking part in a fierce action when he took hold of a hand grenade, pulled the pin and prepared to lob it at a gaggle of attacking Turks in no mans' land. Then, to his horror he slipped.... the grenade fell from his grasp and rolled back into the trench. He dodged into a bay and was safe from the forthcoming blast—but quickly realised his comrades in the trench were not, and the precious seconds were ticking away. Immediately, he abandoned his safe spot and flung himself on to the grenade. A split second later the grenade exploded. His men had been shielded by his body from the blast, but he had been killed instantly. He had made a mistake, but rectified it in the most calculated, brave and final way.

His family shed the tears while from Britain came the VC and from France the Croix de Guerre. Fittingly a plaque on the wall of the Lady Chapel at St John's Parish Church, Blackpool, describes him as a "gallant soldier pure in heart and ever loyal to duty."

It was also against the Turks that another man brought up in Blackpool was awarded the VC.

He was Second Lieutenant Stanley H.P. Boughey whose medal-winning deed came when he was serving in the

1st/4th Royal Scots Fusiliers near Jerusalem. Stan worked for a Blackpool solicitors and he first joined up as a teenager to serve with a medical unit in France, only to be invalided home and discharged. Later, however, he rejoined and was commissioned. In 1917 he was in the thick of Allenby's assaults in the Holy Land.

It was in a Turkish counter-attack near the town of Ramla that the young officer produced his ultimate in valour. The Turks were threatening to over-run the British lines—attacking with bombs and automatic rifles.

Suddenly, Stanley decided to do something about it. Grabbing a clutch of grenades he rushed forward, tossing them among the enemy and smashing their attack.

Just as the Turks were surrendering to the young officer he was hit in the head by a bullet. They struggled to save his life, but two days later he died. He was just 21.

- ★ - ★ -

An Addendum by Bob Dobson

Smith and Boughey were not the only men with Blackpool connections to be awarded the VC. Blackburn lad John Schofield is "claimed" by Blackpool too, as he had attended Arnold School some years before the First World War. The John Schofield story is inseparably linked with the school and the lessons learned there about life— essentially that Virtue lay in valour, courage and manliness, and had honour as its reward. Despite being twice rejected for military service because of defective eyesight, Schofield persisted and received his commission in the Lancashire Fusiliers in 1917 when 25 years old. The following year found him in France leading his men. After personally capturing 20 of the enemy he gathered ten of his men around him and went on to open fire with rifles against machine gun fire at point-blank range. One hundred and twenty eight of the enemy were captured in this brave assault, but Schofield was killed a few minutes later. A tablet to his everlasting memory is displayed with pride in Arnold School.

BLACKPOOL'S WINDMILLS
Some notes compiled by John Clarke
Hoo Hill Windmill, Layton

The name 'Layton'—Laa Ton, means a water course, or peaty water. Around 1180 there was mention of a piece of land on Hoo Hill called "Epiphany Land" and the monks of Cockersand Abbey drew rent from it to provide altar candles.

The mill used to be marked on early navigation charts. It was said that it had canvas spread sails and had the reputation of being the most shapely mill in Lancashire. From its top could be seen the town of Liverpool. In 1583 there was a law suit between the Fleetwood family and John Massey the owner. This mill would be a wooden "post" or "peg" mill. In 1730 an entry in Bispham parish church register, records the death of a child of Cuthbert Helms, miller of Hoo Hill wheel mill.

The last mill on the site (opposite the present Windmill Hotel and at the rear of the shop between Mansfield Road and St Mark's Church) was a wheel mill, brick built with five storeys beneath its cap and sails. An oak beam inside it bore the date 1736, and it is said that the bricks came from a croft which was close to where North Pier now is. The cap or cupola which carried the windshaft and sails was kept facing into the wind by a wheel and chain on the opposite side to the sails. On the mill's South side stood a brick-built drying kiln and a smithy. Thatched cottages for the miller and the blacksmith were next to the pub.

In 1738 Thomas Brade was the miller, so perhaps he had it built.

The mill was struck by lightning in 1879 and again in 1881 with such ferocity that iron work inside melted into a red hot lump which crashed through to the bottom floor. Parts of the sails were scattered all around the field surrounding the mill, and the hoist chain was melted into a ball, which was later found in the cemetery at Layton. Five years later lightning struck again and so badly damaged the mill that it had to be demolished. Its bricks were used to build houses nearby. The last miller was John Gratrix, who had worked there for 50 years. He had 8 children, all born in the thatched cottage next to the mill. The area around the mill had become known as Gratrix's Croft, and St Mark's Church stands on it.

A map of 1786 shows the Layton mill marked as Whole Hill Mill. Perhaps this was corrupted to become Hoo Hill, or perhaps the cartographer got it wrong and it was always Hoo Hill.

Little Marton Mill (Preston New Road)

Yates' map of Lancashire published in 1786 shows this mill.

The present mill was built on the site of an earlier mill in 1838, and was the last mill to be built in the Fylde. The builder was John Whalley and the first miller was George Bagot. 4 storeys high, it had a cellar with an underground passage leading to the drying room. The windshaft was of iron, whereas earlier ones were wooden.

By 1936 the mill had become disused, and was refurbished as a memorial to the local writer Allen Clarke. It became vandalised, and in 1968 a Scout Group became the tenants of the owners, Blackpool Corporation. In 1985, after several attempts at refurbishment, one of the sails blew off, and a great deal of money was spent on it to bring it into first class shape, a symbol of the approach to Blackpool for thousands of motorists who pass it on their way into the town.

Great Marton Mill

This mill was sited on land immediately next to the Oxford Hotel on the Spen Corner side.

It was five storeys high. I don't know when it was built, but it is known that in 1807 it was struck by lightning. It was demolished about 1900.

Another mill, turned by water from Marton Mere was sited near the Oxford junction, and in 1757 it was occupied by Margaret Butler. The waters of the mere must have had a great importance to the early inhabitants. The name "Marton" means (Mere-ton) village by the lake.

★　★　★　★　★

Charles Allen Clarke

MR WINDMILL LAND (Charles Anne Clarke 1863-1935)

His real name was Charles Allen Clarke, yet he chose not to use the Charles, and indeed chose to call himself by many names when writing of his beloved Lancashire. Born in Bolton during the cotton famine, one of 9 children, Clarke's background was one of politics and reading. Working as a child in the cotton factories left its mark on him, not the least of which was a love of the great outdoors. He came to know the moorlands around what he called "Steam Engine Land" very well, though he sought to improve his lot by coming to live in Blackpool. He had graduated from the factory to become a journalist on the Bolton Evening News, and went from there to become a self-employed journalist and publisher. I dare say that no person before or after him wrote more about many aspects of Lancashire than did Allen Clarke. When producing magazines such as *The Blackpool Annual, Teddy Ashton's Journal* and *Teddy Ashton's Lancashire Annual,* he would use many pen-names to hide the fact that he had written most of the contents himself. No other Lancashire writer has used more pen-names.

Clarke's life knew many ups and downs, and the story of it is fascinating indeed. He was an important man in many fields, especially Lancashire literature and politics. His legacy to Blackpudlians are his fine books *Windmill Land* (1916) *More Windmill Land* (1917-18) and *The Story of Blackpool* (1923). These are essential reading for anyone interested in the Blackpool and Fylde of yesteryear.

Clarke lived in Blackpool continuously since 1906 after a few earlier spells here. He came to know and love it and the surrounding countryside, which he explored by bicycle. On his death in 1935, a fund was set up to provide a memorial to the man who coined the phrase *Windmill Land,* and the Marton windmill was chosen as that memorial. Sadly, the plaque affixed to the mill to tell of his work became vandalised and has not been replaced. Think of Allen Clarke as you pass by the mill on Preston New Road. He was a Blackpool champion.

The Blackpool librarian Henry Moore, compiled a list of Clarke's writings in 1972. It can be seen in the town's library.

Boltonian Jack Howarth penned these lines in praise of Allen Clarke, and I am indebted to his wife Margaret, for allowing me to bring them to your notice:-

TEDDY ASHTON

In Steam-Engine Land he was called Teddy Ashton;
He poured out his heart in our Lancashire tongue,
With sketches and ballads, poem and prose,
Wisdom and wit in his song.

Other names, too, as the fancy took him;
What matter so long as the pen run free!
But in Windmill Land he shed the disguise
As the morning mist from the sea.

Part of his heart he had left behind,
Lov'd ones sleeping in Steam-Engine Land;
But the rest he gave to his new-found heaven,
Yielding it up to its lightest demand.

Full thirty-five years he roamed its lanes,
Winter and summer, afoot and awheel,
Singing its praises in weekly rapture,
Pointing a moral, adorning a tale.

From Marton Mere to Freckleton
And o'er the marsh to Lytham,
Whose leafy lanes he knew and loved,
His Dear One riding with him.

Then up the Moss to Plumpton
And on to Weeton's Mill,
Or wheeling off to Inskip
And yet to Cuddy Hill.

From Eccleston to Thistleton,
From Thistleton to Singleton
And over Wyre to Hambleton,
The toll was never done.

Stalmine on to Pilling
And north to Cockersand,
Whose ancient Abbey peasants sought
When famine stalked the land.

No corner of this comely plain,
Not one of all its ways
But stirred his soul to ecstasy,
Each fired its song of praise.

Its quiet, gently-twisting lanes
In milk-white hawthorn frame
No road was straight in Windmill Land
Before the motor came.

Its modest wayside flowers,
The cows that stand and stare,
The never-ending twitter
And fluting in the air.

The rustic ploughman, village bobby,
The children out of school,
Postman, schoolman, tramp and chapman;
He knew and loved them all.

At wayside cottage, trim with roses,
When clock stood ten to three,
Scones with jam or maybe honey,
And heartening pot of tea.

All these he loved with a burning love
That deeply bites and never dies.
"There is no land like Windmill Lane
This side of Paradise."

WHERE ARE THE LADS OF BLACKPOOL?
by Arthur Laycock, about 1915

Where are the lads of Blackpool—
   Those bonny lads of ours—
Who on the Prom. have come and gone
   In happy summer hours?
Where are the stylish dandies,
   The "nuts," the blithesome boys,
The Jacks, the Bills, the Andys,
   Who tasted Blackpool's joys?

Where are the lads of Blackpool?
   They've gone where freemen fight,
There, in sore-stricken Belgium,
   To strike a blow for right.
They've gone—for few were "slackers",
   And none would duty shirk—
They've gone to fight the Prussian,
   The Austrian, and the Turk.

Where are the lads of Blackpool?
   They've 'listed, each brave one;
Gone in the prime of health and strength,
   Each sterling Blackpool son.
Their precious lives they're staking
   That Britain may be free;
That rampant Might shall not kill Right,
   Nor Truth dishonoured be.

Where are the lads of Blackpool?
   They're on the fields of France,
And in the death-strewn Dardanelles,
   Taking the hero's chance.
And some sleep there in Flanders,
   And some lie in the deep;
Mothers and wives in Blackpool
   For these dear brave ones weep.

Where are the lads of Blackpool?
   Ah! ask the lasses all.
Nor wives nor sweethearts held them back
   When came the country's call.
For England, home, and honour
   They left their kindred dear,
And kissed the tears from loving eyes
   As they marched off with a cheer.

Where are the lads of Blackpool?
  They're on the stormy sea,
In ironclad, submarine, and scout,
  Protecting you and me.
They're waiting for the Kaiser
  To put them to the test;
If he comes out there'll be no doubt
  They'll soon put him at rest.

Where are the lads of Blackpool?
  They're all at duty's post.
On land or sea, where'er they be,
  We'll honour our brave host.
We'll toast them all with "Three times three!"
  And when the war is o'er
We'll greet them all right heartily
  On Blackpool's best-loved shore.

BLACKPOOL AND BOB   by Joan Pomfret

Whenever I think of Blackpool I remember Bob, and the many happy afternoons he gave me there as a child. Bob had married the only daughter of our old friend and landlady at Fleetwood, where my parents took me as a baby, and where we went every summer until I was about twelve. He was tall and young and good-looking, and had always made a fuss of me—perhaps because, as it turned out, it was years before he and Ethel had a daughter of their own. I took it for granted then, but I often think now how kind it was of him to bother to take someone else's child to Blackpool! Nevertheless he did this, every summer, and it was one of my annual 'treats' and something I always looked forward to.

I wore one of my 'best' dresses for the occasion, and felt proud to be walking with such a good-looker down Seabank Road and Mount Street to the Tram! The Blackpool trams, then as now, were always rather a thrill and quite different from any other form of transport—and as we rushed along past Rossall and Cleveleys Bob would tell me lots of interesting things and point out the various landmarks and places of interest. I remember him telling me about the two old cannon balls found when Rossall Grange was demolished. These, it was said, were fired from a galleon of the Spanish Armada, which had been driven in a gale onto the Fylde coast—and there was another great storm Bob told me of, in 1833, which left the wreckage of eleven ships on the shore.

We used to get off the tram at Blackpool's North Pier, and join the holiday-makers strolling along the promenade. It was always a lovely day (or so it seems to me now!) and I enjoyed the noise and bustle and the gangs of young people laughing and singing and wearing funny hats inscribed with 'Kiss Me Quick' and 'Hello, Baby!' We would walk as far as The Golden Mile and listen to the 'Hit Tunes'—and on the other side of us the sea would be blue and shining, and Bob would tell me more stories about ships and the fishing trawlers at Fleetwood, and the Isle of Man boats.

Before we went back to Fleetwood we had tea in a café on the front, where I always chose pears and cream, regardless of expense, and after that Bob would always say "I expect you'd like a cake!" and conjure up the most delectable chocolate éclairs or cream buns—he was **so** kind to me! I only remember one regrettable incident (when I thought I'd locked myself in a cubicle at 'The Ladies'—but even then, a kind woman spoke to me through the door and instructed me how to slide the bolt open!) They were Red Letter Days—those afternoons in Blackpool with Bob—and because of them Blackpool has always had a warm place in my affections. Strangely enough, when so many other towns have changed out of recognition, it still stays the place I remember walking in with him in those days before the war, and I can **still** thrill to a walk on the Pier or a trip through the Tower!

After tea we would walk back to the North Pier and stand in the queue for the tram again. I sometimes imagine us there—that tall fair young man and the little girl in white socks and a blue dress—and I try to recapture the intense pleasure of those summer afternoons long ago!

"Did she behave herself"? Mother would ask when we got back to Fleetwood. "Was she a good girl"? And Bob, bless him, would reply "Joan's **always** a good girl at Blackpool!" I believe I was—I only hope his own little girl, when she came, had the same lovely times he gave to me!

The Diary of Thomas Butler of Kirkstall Forge, Yorkshire, an early visitor to Blackpool (1796)

Extracted by W. John Smith, A.T.D., F.S.A.

Mardi 26 Juillet 1796

Very early we set off from Garstang to Blackpool—distant 20 Miles—arrived to Breakfast. And took up our Lodgings at Smiths Hotel—the Lane Ends. a very comfortable House it is—the Provisions are Good—the Beds comfortable—and the Attendance very regular—and every other accommodation excellent. and the Charges not very extravagant.

We spent 14 Days at this place in the utmost harmony; every day bro^t fresh pleasures—the Scenes were constantly diversified by the Company coming and going—We were met with people of all descriptions, Young & Old, Rich & Poor, Sensible & Foolish,—Good tempered and bad tempered, proud and affable, agreable and disagreable.

Our Mornings were spent in Eating our Breakfast, Reading, Bathing; Dressing—Our Afternoons in Walking, and our Evenings in Conversation—I had other amusement—with the Gentlemen—Bowls, and Billiards—with the Ladies Drafts and Cards.

But my Greatest Happiness was with my Ann—Sometimes in rural walks in the Fields—at other times alone on the Sands—And many a time in her Room upstairs, for many an hour have I enjoyed her Sweet Conversation; have squeezed her Lovely form to my Heart. and imprinted upon her ruby Lips a Thousand Kisses:—Such were the Days we past at Blackpool.

5th Augt 1796.

To Will Horner

I am now at Blackpool where I have been for 10 days—along with thy Mother, Ann Porter and my Sister Lyd; A heavy shower of rain has just drove me from the Bowling Green, I have won 2½—I ran upstairs into my room, and a pleasant room it is it looks upon the Sea—the vast Atlantic rolls its proud waves under my Window, a mighty West Wind makes the Billows foam and roar terribly,—I cannot walk out so I will write to thee—Oh! Oh! sayest thou I am much obliged to thee for writing to me when thou canst do nothing else—But hold hold I could do something else—for the Ladies want me to read to them—I have refused—I prefer writing to thee.

We left Kendal and posted forwards, through Burton, Lancaster and Garstang to Blackpool, where we now are, and from whence I write this: Here we are very comfortably situated, Our Minds are disposed to be happy and we are happy—We need not the foreign aid of Company to make us more so, for our Happiness centers in ourselves, because we love each other.—We have excellent accommodations, the company consists of about 20—All chearful and merry —We purpose spending about a fortnight here, we bathe frequently in the sea, & hope all of us by this means to add to the Length of the days of our Lives, I do not know how many Years.

While I now write the vast Atlantic rolls its proud waves under my Window; 'Tis about high water, and a brisk Gale of Wind sets in from the West, which makes the foaming Billows rise to a prodigious height with a hoarse & terrible roar.

The Diary of Rev. William Thornber, a Blackpool historian

Extracted by W. John Smith, A.T.D., F.S.A.

These brief extracts are from the entries for 1861. The original diary is in Mr Smith's possession. Blackpool-born, Mr Smith is a local historian of high reputation now living in Middleton, Manchester. He is the author of *Blackpool; A sketch of its growth, 1740-1851* (Transactions of the Lancashire and Cheshire Antiquarian Society, 1959)

1861

June 19th Wednesday. The iron church is opened on Sunday next. A Mr Wainright from Eccles and latterly from St James, Manchester (my old friend Hoberst incumbent there). He is said to be eloquent; he is tall with regular features. He gives not the idea of talent but "Funti nulla fides &c."

I believe I before-hand saw what Blackpool might be, and pushed improvements amid many hindrences especially from the farmers openly at the Vestry Meetings held in the old house of Richard Warbrick overseer in Chapel street on a Clay floor. These gents forced on us the Board of Health, instead of a Private one, in order to be do-nothings. Latterly they are scouted but by the need squatters are in power again.

The Chairman Robt. Rawcliffe of Layton Hawes representts Clifton can just read, makes pot hooks and ladles but cannot spell a word. First saw money (dubloons) at the wreck of the Boltona hence his nickname—this tale is corroborated and fully believed. He is now an usurer and task hunter. His notes are a treat and handed round as a laughing stock.

The next is Thos. Fenton of ffoxhall a small ratepayer one of the roughest of men—may read, knows not addition, he has learnt to write his name. He is however an honest man and shrewd.

The third is W. Watson, yeoman and farmer on the Hawes, the estate belonging to him, three brothers and a sister. I should have bought it for the church. It has doubled itself. He is **dateless**—a fool, senseless and a mop stock. He can just write but his sister has born a child to him. Oh!

The 4 is Mr Wade called **Tacking End** a house builder just now on borrowed money, a teetotaller who makes it religion and political dissenter. In learning he is a **dullart**.

The 5 is John Moore, chemist and German (Revoe). He was a Moss Moore. Sauny his great grandfather being Hesketh's bailiff there when that now valuable tract of land offered to him at *(omitted)* He is a good fellow, too fond like his father of a wee drop of the crature—sings "I love a glass of good beer, I does, I does." "Good ale thou art my darling". But he troubles himself with the Board affairs about once in six months.

The 6th is Mr Smith of Rumbler's Hill, a kind man but a political dissenter—a scraper yet rich—a builder to sell. He is a novus homo (upstart) nourished by Cotton. He has got money and keeps it. He does no harm if he does no good. Every month he faithfully sees his friends' bills paid with this his only speech. "Mr .... account should be paid for he is coming over." Kind, soft, ignorante man, your talk never distressed your audience like W. Watson's "hownsoever", "nevertheless" and "mark my words." "If reet be reet let us do it, bod if wrang, why, let us shut up" it did one execution.

The seventh is John Eccleston a doll man but calling himself a jeweller now. John is a charitable man but very illiterate. Uses words by bushels but so sifted that little corn is left. He will talk especially if a little corned— John is proficient in bad grammar and spelling. A lucky stroke made John, who never hoped to attain local honour. He was on the spree one day—his partener sent the bell round for him as lost. John heard and indignant demanded a dissolution of partnership, then a toss was thrown for the shed standing place, he won, borrowed £150, paid it off the same year and prospered. His steady partner now his brother in law lives in a small shop of his, doing but little business in Talbot Road.

The last is Augustus Adolfus Viener, a German Jewish family. His uncle now a Xan (Christian) made his fortune here as a Jews harp seller, doll man or jeweller. He looks down since he built a nice cottage at South Shore, on those who carried a pack with him. He however is a moral man, kind but passionate, and charitable. His pride I suppose is a right pride. Died in a mad house.

A.A.V. was elected by the political dissenters by one vote, no trouble spared. He took his seat at the head of the table, reads the letters for Chairman to which I objected by saying "If the Chairman cannot read them pray do let the clerk." Speaks well, sensibly but pompously, thinking, "I am monarch of all I survey." He rules, for he has knowledge of a kind, whilst the rest are nearly **gormless** in toto. Out of doors he rules **home-wards.** Do this and the official obeys. Last summer he wipt a boy for touching a whip at his door but the father seized him by the beard and dragged him down the street. He lives in style in appearance. One of his sisters is talented, a publisher of novels. He is a puppy in dress, in manner, in talk, in carriage, yet, I believe him to be clever. Time and some edges sand-papered he may be useful. "Nature which has given us our bodily organs has also bestowed pride to spare us the pains of being aware of our imperfections".

I wish thee well, Viener, but divest thyself of that self love which is the greatest of all flatterers.

Ere this we should have had a proper set of Commissioners if we had followed a friend's advice, viz. eight mopstocks painted with divers colours and yearly labelled, had not another influential gentleman began to canvass for subscriptions towards an Anti-scandal Society, the members being protected from libellous attacks. I have signed my name to the mutual protection and prosecutory bond.

June 20th Thursday. The papers give the account of the bloody discraceful fight of Hurst and Mace for Championship. "Renew the prize ring!!!" says the Times. After this slaughter what decent man can be seen at a fight! Yet I loved the science of self defence. The sword to the gentleman as the needle to a woman. Not wrangle to be bold to give offence; but a manlike confidence. I am acknowledged to be strong, to have a good courage and daring; few men once could cope with me in any athletic excercises, yet who never knew me to provoke a quarrel. Confidence in our strength only makes a coward an agressor. I could box, wrestle, fence, single stick, swim &c. but fighting I abhorres lest forced to defend myself and then......Remember I was a youth in the French War when most boys rushed to be a sailor or soldier. I once thought, I could have wished, to have been a warrior. I think better now.

★　★　★　★　★

Blackpool in 1856, drawn by an artist for the *Illustrated News*.

Probably the earliest known pictures of Blackpool, drawn by W.H.
Bartlett and engraved by J.C. Armytage about 1830.

Raikes Hall, the seat of Daniel Hornby Esq.

In 1881/82 was erected a new branch of the Manchester and County Bank on Lytham Street. Built of Longridge stone, 45 feet long and 36 feet to the top of the main cornice. The 150 sq yards of land had been bought that year for £2,000, and in 1897 a further 188 square yards were bought for £4,000. The bank was therefore built in two parts at a total cost, including fittings and furnishings, of £8,280. The Manchester & County Bank was to become merged with the County Bank in 1935, then later that became The District Bank, then (1961) The National Provincial Bank, and in 1970 that bank became The National Westminster. Lytham Street became Corporation Street in 1929, at a time when a total of 76 Blackpool streets were re-named by Act of Parliament.

THOMAS TYLDESLEY OF FOX HALL   by Bob Dobson

Thomas Tyldesley (1657-1715) was of the finest Lancashire Catholic stock. The Tyldesleys had been landed gentry since Tudor times, and even before that had bourne arms in London and Lancashire. Thomas' grandfather, Sir Thomas, had fought for Charles I and had been slain at Wigan Lane in 1651. His father, Edward, won the favour of Charles II and had hoped that his King would help restore the fortunes of a family impoverished through their loyalty to the Stuart line. This was not to be, and when his father died, Thomas inherited debts as well as land. Incidentally, the family got its name from the township of Tyldesley in South Lancashire.

Though probably educated in a Catholic school in France. Thomas rarely moved outside Lancashire. There is no reason to suppose that his life would be much different to the picture he paints of it in the diary he kept during the last three years of his life. Many years later, about 1870, this manuscript diary was discovered in the possession of a Mr Parkinson at Myerscough, and passed into the possession of Anthony Hewitson, a Preston printer, journalist and historian, who, along with Joseph Gillow of Lancaster edited, interpreted and published the diary in 1873. It makes fascinating reading.

To understand Thomas, it is necessary to understand the times in which he lived. England's Catholics were persecuted for sticking to their faith and their Church services were held in secret in private homes. Queen Anne ruled, but there was such strength of pro-Catholic feeling that in a few year's time (1715) men were to ride South to fight for the restoration of the Jacobite line, which would restore the Catholic Church as the Establishment. In Lancashire, there were many landed families of Catholic persuasion. The Tyldesleys met them regularly in their houses, at weddings, funerals and the Assizes.

Thomas owned several houses on his estates in the Fylde and throughout Amounderness Hundred. The two at which he spent most time were Myserscough Lodge, his ancestral home, and Fox Hall, built by his father as a hunting lodge of cobblestones from the Blackpool shore. Renovated and rebuilt, it now sees use as the Foxhall Hotel. Being a Catholic, the law prevented Thomas from holding offices, so perhaps this was why he had so much "free time".

Remember, this was the Blackpool before the railway and the trippers. Much Fylde land was owned by the

Tyldesleys, and Thomas drew the rents from tenant farmers bearing such names as Gornall, Butler and Jolly. His cousin, Charles Rigby, lived at Layton and he regularly met the Allens from Rossall Hall.

Throughout Thomas' diary, he writes of hours spent in ale-houses, (often till 1 o'clock in the morning) "in good company". He doesn't mention much drunkenness, and makes special reference to "usqubath" (whisky), a new unusual liquor. Port had not yet arrived in England, though there was ale, claret, white wine, brandy, cider, sack and canary. In the area between Lancaster and Preston there were hostelries a-plenty where a man and his horse could eat, drink and sleep.

Thomas and his wife—she wasn't mentioned much in the diary—travelled everywhere on horse-back, and the horse featured in a great love of his life—hunting. He kept a fox kennelled at Fox Hall, perhaps in case none could be found in the Fylde fields, or more likely to show visitors, or perhaps to reflect the house name. He found deer in Fylde woodlands and kept hounds for the purpose. He referred to himself in his diary as "old Dog Lad". He gave guests oysters, presumably from the Blackpool beds. Those guests at Fox Hall would certainly include Catholic priests.

However, the joviality, sport, gaming and drinking are all secondary to the love Thomas had for his faith—the largest factor in his life. He recorded confession as "X" and rode to arrive late at night at houses for prayers. He makes many entries referring to priests and prayers, and saw fit to take notice when young Tom Carus, a member of one of a strong Catholic family attended the Established Church one morning and again in the afternoon.

John Marsh & Son (Blackpool) Ltd
and
Blackpool Van Transport Ltd

Blackpool's Leading Hauliers

197 Midgeland Road
Blackpool FY4 5HJ

Tel: (0253) 62281/2

This poem in praise of Blackpool was written by Samuel Laycock's son Arthur Laycock, probably around 1914. Arthur became Blackpool's first Socialist town councillor.

BLACKPOOL FOR ME!

Yo' may talk abeawt Douglas or Morecambe,
  Llandudno or Southport—so gay,
Yo' may crack up yore Scarbro' or Brighton,
  But Blackpool beats th' lot ony day.

Yo' get say-sick when sailing to th' Island;
  At Morecambe you just fall asleep;
At stylish Llandudno or Southport
  Yo' parade abeawt th' place like lost sheep.

T'other places, well, they, can't be reckoned,
  They're scarcely on th' map, do yo' see.
Blackpool's th' place every hour, minute, second;
  Blackpool's th' place for fun, frolic, and sea.

Here yo' con enjoy life i' rare fashion;
  See th' best entertainments in th' land;
Walk th' promenades—miles long, near th' wayter,
  Or watch th' youngsters diggin' in th' sand.

Yo' con laugh, dance and sing, sleep and eyt, too;
  Yo' con just enjoy life as yo' should;
So come here an' join us at Blackpool,
  It will do yo' a rare power o' good.

BLACKPOOL'S FIRST TOWN COUNCIL

Blackpool was incorporated in May 1876, and the town was divided into six wards. The following is a list of the first Town Council:-

CLAREMONT WARD
T. McNaughtan (Alderman)
William Bailey
J. Braithwaite
Leslie Jones

TALBOT WARD
Thomas Lambert Masheter (Alderman)
Thomas Challoner
Richard Marshall
John Fisher

BANK HEY WARD
William Henry Cocker (Alderman and Mayor)
George Ormerod
John Coulston
Henry Fisher

BRUNSWICK WARD
J.E. Banks Cocker (Alderman)
Robert Mather
George Bonny
J.W. Mycock

FOXHALL WARD
John Hardman (Alderman)
Dr. Alfred Anderson
James Blundell Fisher
Robert Bickerstaff

WATERLOO WARD
Francis Parnell (Alderman)
Richard Gorst
Lawrence Hall
George Sharples

Looking at these names, consider how many of them are so very closely related to the development of the town, and how many of them live on in street names—Cocker Square, Banks Street, Braithwaite Street, Fisher Street, Bonny Street. A series of "pen-pictures" of these men appeared in the pages of the "Blackpool Gazette" in 1876 under the pen of a Mr Hunter, and were printed in book form at the end of that year.

1876-1879	William Henry Cocker
1879-1880	Francis Parnell
1880	Thomas McNaughtan
1880-1883	Henry Hall
1883-1884	John Hardman
1884-1885	William Henry Cocker
1885-1886	Thomas McNaughtan
1886-1887	William Henry Cocker
1887-1889	James Fish
1889-1891	Sir John Bickerstaffe
1891-1892	Henry Buckley
1892-1894	James Cardwell
1894-1896	Frederick Henry Parkinson
1896	James Cardwell
1896-1897	James Ward
1897-1898	Robert Butcher Mather
1898-1899	Joseph Heap
1899-1900	George C. Kingsbury
1900-1901	Thomas Houldsworth Smith
1901-1902	James Howarth
1902-1903	James Heyes
1903-1904	Gilbert Blundell
1904-1905	Joseph Brodie
1905-1906	William Henry Broadhead
1906-1907	Samuel Hill
1907-1908	James Battersby
1908-1910	Thomas Fielding
1910-1911	William Henry Broadhead
1911-1912	John Collins
1912-1913	Milton Gough Wilde
1913-1914	James Dewhurst
1914-1915	William Cartledge
1915-1916	Richard Holt
1916-1919	Sir Lindsay Parkinson
1919-1920	Eli Hey Howe
1920-1921	Charles William Callis
1921-1922	David Dickinson
1922-1924	Henry Brooks
1924-1925	Thomas Pilling Fletcher
1925-1926	Thomas Bickerstaffe
1926-1927	Robert Fenton
1927-1928	Tom Gallon Lumb
1928-1929	John Potter
1929-1930	George William Gath
1930-1931	Peter James Tomlinson
1931-1932	Leonard Newsome
1932-1933	Thomas Fenton
1933-1934	Charles Edward Tatham
1934-1935	George Whittaker
1935-1936	Walter Newman
1936-1937	William Sandiford Ashton
1937-1938	John Robert Quayle
1938-1939	William Rostron Duckworth
1939-1940	Edward Stevenson
1940-1941	Harry Allan Thickett
1941-1942	Daniel Jennings Bailey

1942-1943	Percy Round OBE
1943-1944	Jacob Parkinson
1944-1945	John William Roberts
1945-1946	Frank Iddeson Nickson MBE
1946-1947	John Robert Frank Hill MM
1947	Rhodes William Marshall
1947	John Anderson
1948-1949	John Robert Furness
1949-1950	Alfred Salisbury
1950-1951	Rhodes William Marshall
1951-1952	Joseph Hill
1952-1953	Peter Fairhurst
1953-1954	Edwin Smith
1954-1955	Will Ogden
1955-1956	Charles Dunn
1956-1957	Herbert Henson
1957-1958	Harold Grimbledeston BEM
1958-1959	Joseph Parker
1959-1960	Ernest Alfred Machin CBE
1960-1961	Thomas Bagot Fairclough
1961-1962	Clifford Cross
1962-1963	Joseph Shepherd Richardson CBE
1963-1964	John Herbert Smythe
1964-1965	Albert Ashworth
1965-1966	Tom Joyce
1966-1967	Robert Brierley
1967-1968	Leslie Pilkington
1968-1969	Jean Robinson CBE
1969-1970	Albert Edward Stuart
1970-1971	James Henry Hessey MBE
1971-1972	Horace Samuel Arthur Ward
1972-1973	Edmund Ernest Wynne
1973-1974	Raymond Jacobs
1974-1975	Walter Uriah Robinson
1975-1976	Harold Leslie Hoyle MBE
1976-1977	Alfred Hudson
1977-1978	Cyril Nuttall MBE
1978	Cyril Lowe
1978-1979	Margaret Riley
1979-1980	Robert Charles Dewhirst
1980-1981	Daniel Collin Hanson
1981-1982	James Blake
1982-1983	Thomas Waddicot Percival
1983-1984	Marjorie Hoggard
1984-1985	Cyril Lowe
1986-1987	John Landor
1987-1988	Leo Pomfret

TWOPENCE FOR FISH FAT!   by Stan Whittaker

It is more pleasing to travel hopefully than to arrive, the old saying goes. This being so, consider what an immense source of pleasure it must have been to countless numbers of people en-route for Blackpool to have *arrived* at their destination while still afar off, merely from catching their first glimpse of Blackpool's famous Tower at long range.

Today the family car and high-powered motorcoach rushes young and old in the direction of the seaside at a phenomenal speed. Trippers are ceasing to enjoy the thrill of unexpectedly spotting the Tower from some viewpoint miles away across the Fylde, as once they did.

But the joyful game of Blackpool Tower-spotting is not altogether dead, thank goodness. "Theer it is, see, ower yonder!" the children—and even grown-ups—yell, upon seeing the 518 feet tall structure beckoning them to the town.

Journeying by train, the holidaymakers' first glimpse of the Tower is usually to be obtained on the line between Kirkham and Lytham, at Moss Side. On the Preston-to-Poulton-be-Fylde length the spectacle arises as their trains cruise along that stretch of track just beyond Weeton signal box.

"We'se no'an be long now, afoor we're theer," a parent will be heard to reassure his or her excited youngsters. Of such stuff—and lots of other delights—are Blackpool holidays made.

Blackpool Tower-spotting has been going on for years. What has been going on much longer is the celebrated Blackpool landlady in business providing the holiday-makers with their accommodation.

These days, the trade is done in "private hotels." Originally, the premises were lodging houses or company houses. From being conducted by "landladies" they have come to be directed by a so-called "proprietress."

An amiable 74 year-old South Shore lady who prefers not to be named remembers the lodging house era sixty years ago extremely well. Her recollections make interesting reading. Particularly as the family were in the trade no fewer than 34 years.

Up to the outbreak of World War I, visitors paid two shillings (10p) per night. By 1919, after peace had returned, the price had doubled. Milk would be charged for at 4p for the week: use of the salt, pepper and mustard (described on the bill as "cruet") cost a further 2p, while the equivalent of 2½ new pence was levied for the fat in which were fried the fillets that went with the chips.

Traditionally, Lancashire families working in the cotton mills, would have a day out to Blackpool early in the year. This was to book up their "lodgings" well in advance of their annual "Wakes" week.

They would knock on the door, asking: "Can you take us for 't week in July?" Once the arrangement had been made and my mother had fixed them up with a friendly cup of tea they would take the children, with buckets and spades, to spend the rest of the day on the sands. One reason being that they did not have sufficient money to go and eat in a cafe.

At the company house in question, up to 40 visitors at a time could be accommodated. Two attic bedrooms provided sleeping room for as many as 12. "Six youths to a room thought nothing of sleeping three-in-a-bed," explains the South Shore lady.

Blackpool lodging houses, sixty years ago, could offer no such luxuries as hot and cold water in all bedrooms. Nor would there be a bathroom. One lavatory on the landing had to serve all 40 visitors. For the holidaymakers there were jugs of water and basins on the bedroom chest of drawers at which to wash themselves.

A familiar personality in the house throughout each season would be "the girl."

Usually, she would be one of the daughters of a Yorkshire miner's family. Times were hard in the pits. These girls would leave home round about Whitsuntide and get work for the summer as domestics in the boarding-houses.

They returned each year and had the reputation of being good workers. They were paid ten shillings (50p) a week and 'all found'—bed and food provided; making their way home at the end of September.

A working day began at 6.15 a.m. Either our informant or "the girl" would begin by "doing out" the dining room and scrubbing the front doorstep—to include washing the flagstones to the front pavement! At the same time, the kitchen was full of activity as preparations for feeding the 40 hungry visitors got into full gear.

"One of my first jobs of the day was dusting the furniture in the dining room and sitting room. Under-standably, there was always plenty of washing-up to be tackled, first thing, remembering that there was the previous suppertime's crockery to be put through the water. At suppertime, whoever wanted would be served with a cup of tea, coffee or cocoa (price slightly more than 1p per cup)."

41

Time obliterates so many memories that it is only by chatting with such as our friend, this South Shore lady, that one comes to understand the subtle difference between those two renowned Blackpool personalities, the "companyhouse-keeper" and the lodginghouse-keeper.

Indeed, there was a finely-drawn demarcation line between their respective activities.

Your companyhouse-keeper, apparently, was the woman whose catering for holidaymakers comprised sleeping accommodation and "all found," with food provided. This was at the "magnificent" price of seven shillings and sixpence a day (38p). It included breakfast, dinner, tea, and a supper comprised of cold meat sandwiches from the mid-day roast.

"Every meal was a gigantic feed. Blackpool's sea breezes gave the honest-to-goodness working folk of Lancashire and Yorkshire some very big appetites, as is the case today. Visitors to the town liked full value for their money by way of food."

The "lodginghouse-keeper" was the landlady who took in holidaymakers merely to "lodge"..... that is to say, they slept on the premises but provided their own food—for this to be cooked by their landlady, as required.

There is the tale of a Darwen couple who were in the tripe-dressing business in their home town. When "Wakes" week came round, father collected together his very large family for them to catch the train to Blackpool to spend the next seven days at a seaside lodginghouse.

On Darwen station, a friendly railway porter enquired of the head of the family. "What's tha getten theer, in't big tin trunk, George, among aw't rest o' thi luggage."

"Tripe," was the prompt reply, "Eno'oo for 't week, for seven 'on us."

As a lodginghouse-keeper, whose customers took in their own eatables, a landlady used to supply them with their potatoes, peas, cabbage and carrots, plus a pudding, usually rice or sago. Otherwise, each family staying on the premises (usually the wife) bought from the local shops each day its required meat for the next day.

Refrigerators and freezers were unknown, so the holidaymaking housewife did not buy-in for further ahead than tomorrow. Each family's meat would have a ticket bearing the family name affixed to it, in readiness for it being deposited in the oven for cooking.

Two o'clock in the afternoon was the worst hour of toil for the landlady and her husband, and, of course, any of her daughters assisting in running the premises, along with "the girl."

This was when the visitors (Blackpool holidaymakers had not come to be known as "guests" in those days) had finished their hefty, mid-day meal.

"Two o'clock meant us all setting to the task of washing-up after 40 people. We ourselves had eaten before the visitors came trooping in for dinner," explained our informant. "We ate at about half-past 11 in the back kitchen."

Saturday mornings brought a special routine seen on no other morning in the companyhouse or boardinghouse. "It was my job on a Saturday morning, while the visitors were packing their luggage before going home, to go round all the bedrooms. First, I cleaned the candlestick in each bedroom of its overflowed wax, then fixed in new candles.

Sheets and pillowcases on every bed had to be stripped off and replaced with snowy-white ones. As for Friday nights, they were also something special .... the evening on which a member of the family must not forget to water the aspidistra, washing its leaves down with cold tea.

And if all the foregoing reads like a catalogue of sheer, hard work, that is what being a Blackpool lodginghouse or companyhouse-keeper faced every season, sixty years ago.

Only after sweating it out for six gruelling seasons in an establishment could you count upon having gained a "connection", a constant flow of regular summer visitors. Today and yesteryear, this has never been an occupation for the faint-hearted or the work-shy.

THE EARLY LABOUR MOVEMENT IN BLACKPOOL
(1885 to 1914)
Percy Patrick Hall, J.P., Freeman of Blackpool

The heroic period of working-class struggle was over before Blackpool developed. The right to form trade unions, the right to vote, the right to advocate an alternative economic system had been won earlier and elsewhere.

The Co-operative Movement was the first local effort. In 1885 John Leach stood up in the porters' room at Central Station and persuaded his fellow railwaymen to form a Blackpool Co-operative Society. Fleetwood, Kirkham and Preston had already got them. With a capital of 5d and promises of £40 the Co-op began in a rented shop in Corporation Street with a man, a boy and a grocery basket.

The most important event in the history of Blackpool's Labour Movement was the formation of the United Trades and Labour Council of Blackpool and District. The first meeting was held in the Wellington Hotel on October 5th, 1891. Six societies came together, believing that Unity is Strength. They demanded a Fair Wages Clause for Corporation contracts, the abolition of the Aldermanic Compact and began to find out how working men could be elected to the Town Council and become magistrates. Those with influence were middle-class land speculators, shop keepers and builders. Men of little culture but of mighty power.

The intellectual ferment of the 1880's is not well documented, as no minute books have survived, but the memory of the oldest members passed on to those who are now old is our source. Arthur Laycock, son of Samuel Laycock, the Blackpool dialect poet, told Abraham Fielding in 1903 that he had belonged to a Fabian Group in 1888. The existence of the Blackpool Fabian Group is confirmed in Pease's *History of the Fabian Society*. The Group met to discuss alternatives to capitalism. They were not Marxists: they believed that all social problems could be solved by gathering the facts, analysing them and reaching conclusions. The Webbs were their mentors through the Fabian Essays and Tracts. The Fabian Group and some members of the Trades and Labour Council founded a branch of Keir Hardie's Independent Labour Party in 1893, whose main purpose was to fight elections with *Labour* candidates, though the word *Socialist* was often used. They organised the Sands Meetings at which Labour speakers of national calibre addressed the holiday crowds.

A few years later, a new group called the *Blackpool Clarion Fellowship* built its own Guild Room at the end of Woodland Grove. It was referred to as the Woodland Cabin. They built it with their own hands. It stood where, by historical coincidence, the Fylde Art Society now stands in Wilkinson Avenue. It lasted until Stanley Park was built in 1926 when it had become a tool-shed for Hobson the market gardener. Its members were artists, thinkers, poets and socialists. Joseph Parr, the first secretary of the Trades Council, Thomas Smith, the plumber and first Chairman of the Blackpool Labour Party, Conrad Morley, artist of the Blackpool Herald whose election posters became classic. Fellowship was their inspiration and the beams of the Cabin were adorned with carvings, among which was *Fellowship is life: lack of it is death*. They studied Tolstoy and Ruskin, formed a branch of the Clarion Cycling Club and took an allotment on Central Drive to prove the dignity of labour. The Fellowship died with the pioneers and the remnant joined the Independent Labour Party.

The progenitor, the original, the stabiliser of the Labour Movement was The Trades and Labour Council that has continued until the present day with only one short break at the turn of the century when the Trades Council died in sympathy with the old Queen. There was no meeting of the Trades Council from January, 1901 until April, 1903 when a new start was made. During the interval, the Clarion Fellowship and the Independent Labour Party put up a Socialist candidate in Talbot Ward and were successful. Dick Greenwood was the candidate. He became the proprietor of Greenwood's Laundry. He was the first Labour Councillor. The Trades Council was suffering from amnesia.

Only two unions were common to the old and new Trades Councils, the Printers and the Railway Servants. A new union, unique to Blackpool, was the Sandsmen's Union that tried to unite the competing seasonal entertainers on the Blackpool sands. Albert Williams of the Tailors' Society used the old minute book so that the record of the first ten years was preserved and he called on Joseph Parr to address them on the past. Parr was by then the Manager of the Union Printers in Charnley Road, a co-operative run by the Printers Union to employ the printers who had been dismissed for forming a trade union. The Trades Council submitted his name to the Duchy of Lancaster hoping that he might be made a magistrate and they helped the I.L.P. to promote a candidate in Brunswick Ward. They failed in both.

In 1905 and 1906 Arthur Laycock of the I.L.P. fought two annual elections and two by-elections in Foxhall Ward. In 1906 he was returned, the second Labour Councillor though he owed more to the I.L.P. and the Clarion Fellowship than to the Trades Council. He stood as a Socialist. The poll was:-

FOXHALL WARD

Arthur Laycock (Socialist)	1073
William Eaves (Conservative)	624
John Laurie (Conservative)	505

Foxhall being a two member ward, Laycock and Eaves were returned. In the same year Joseph Parr was appointed a magistrate.

This double success encouraged the Trades Council to invite the I.L.P. and the Clarion Fellowship to a special meeting held in the Coronation Street Schools (now the Theatre of Magic) to put Labour representation on a sound footing. There was no agreement among the unions to support the formation of a Labour Representation Committee and a letter was sent to James Ramsay Macdonald, declining to join. He must have been surprised that a Trades and Labour Council was still using such an archaic term, for the Labour Party had been formed for some time.

Two applications were received for electoral support for the November elections of 1907, one from C. Allen Clarke and the other from Jim Pablo. Allen Clarke was the journalist and writer who had been an I.L.P. member for years and Jim Pablo was an asphalt layer with Blackpool Corporation, a free-thinking trade unionist, whom good fortune turned into the wealthiest ice-cream merchant of his day. *"When in debt, ask Jim Pablo"* was the tag many years later. He received the support of the Trades Council because he was a member but Clarke did not. Both were at the bottom of the poll, a defeat attributed to the deliberate abstention of the Tories and a combination of public house tipplers and Liberal tee-totallers.

On the 27th June, 1908 the three bodies tried again to set up a *Labour Representation Committee* and succeeded. They sent off the affiliation fee of 15/- and Ramsay Macdonald duly acknowledged it, asking if the new Party would like to nominate a name for the parliamentary panel. The officers were:-

President Thomas Smith, Operative Plumbers Society
Secretary Jim Pablo, Gas Workers and General Union
Treasurer William Atherton, Operative Stonemasons Union

Ezra Ford, Abraham Fielding, William Stirzaker and John Blacow made up the Committee.

The Blackpool Labour Party was born, but true to its character, not without dissent. The Railwaymen, the Postmen and the Printers voted against its formation because they were afraid of their jobs, the Railwaymen because of the Osbourne Judgement, the Postmen because of their position as servants under the Crown and the Printers because they would have no truck with socialists.

In 1909 Arthur Laycock lost his seat. A propaganda sheet entitled *The Labour Advocate* was distributed by the new Blackpool Labour Party. Laycock was its editor, Conrad Morley the artist who designed the block at the head of the paper and the Blackpool Printers did the work. They distributed a thousand copies each month. Typical of their propaganda was an article which contrasted the treatment of Officers in the Corporation and their labourers. The Chief Officers were to receive £100 per annum each as an increase while the gas workers application for ½d rise an hour increase was refused as extravagant. The cost of running the paper was too much for the weak Labour Party, so the Trades Council took the paper under its wing.

At the end of the 1911 season the Corporation sacked seven tramwaymen for belonging to a trade union. The Trades and Labour Council declared war. In March, 1912 a Mass Meeting was called to consider reprisals and the secretary, Ezra Ford proposed writing to all the trade unions and working men's institutes to boycott Blackpool as a conference centre. A special edition of two thousand *Labour Advocates* was distributed by members in the centre of the town and a meeting was held outside the Bloomfield Road football-ground before the game. Despite the boycott, the coal miners held their conference but made amends by sending their General Secretary to intercede with the Mayor and Corporation. All to no avail: the tramwaymen sought work in Halifax.

In 1913, delegates attended a conference on the Workers Educational Association. They reported so favourably that the Council formed the Blackpool Branch and its officers became the officers of the W.E.A. As usual there was dissent. Opposition to the W.E.A. was voiced by those purists who believed that Adult Education that was subsidised by University and the Board of Education must be tainted. A resolution of July, 1914 calling for a General Strike if war was declared was more heroic than practical. The Council met on 5th August, 1914. There were twelve delegates present! The Expeditionary Force was already crossing the Channel. The War was on.

LIBS WHA HAE   by Harry Hodgkinson

Could Edgar Wallace have become Liberal M.P. for Blackpool at the 1931 election?

A view from a local newspaper reporter's desk at the time suggests the answer—just possibly, but on three conditions: that he back the National Government without qualifications; that he did his homework on the Lancashire cotton industry; and that his image could be tailored to match the austere Nonconformity of his principal supporters.

Blackpool's politics have always been something of a paradox. It scoops up its livelihood with the left hand but votes with the right. It depends on the Lancashire working class, but visitors don't have votes. Those who do are typically boardinghouse-keepers wanting to keep the rates down, and retired people trying to make ends meet on a fixed income.

So politically Blackpool has remained as impregnably Conservative as a dormitory seat in the deep blue South.

With one exception: in 1923, for a single year and to its own astonishment, Blackpool went Liberal. When the returning Officer sent up a red rocket instead of the expected blue one, the townspeople thought his staff must be colour-blind. The alternative was to suppose that the laws of nature were ceasing to work.

This victory was the last rally of the Free Traders, galvanised by the premature Conservative call for a revenue tariff. Former cotton weavers and their wives now "taking in" summer holidaymakers in Blackpool, joined commuting merchants and millowners from St. Annes to defeat, of all people, a Tory Admiral of the Stanley family.

The Conservatives learned their lesson. Nationally, they dropped tariffs. Locally, they adopted Sir Walter de Frece, husband of the male impersonator Vesta Tilley and himself a theatrical impresario. He knew the entertainment business from the inside. He had money, a title, and the rather obtrusive good looks that rightly go with both in the popular imagination. It was the ideal formula for bringing the Blackpool votes back to the fold.

When the '31 crisis election was sprung on the country, though, de Frece was no longer available, and even he had sat towards the end as a minority member, polling less than the combined Liberal and Labour vote.

The Conservatives found themselves with an unknown ex-Army captain called Clifford Charles Alan Lawrence

Erskine-Bolst, FRGS, and there was no Labour man in prospect. Small wonder that the Liberal caucus began to sniff the beguiling scent of euphoria.

Made up for the most part of small tradesmen, its ideal of a candidate was a non-drinking, high-minded Nonconformist, used to public speaking (most probably from a pulpit), who had served a long apprenticeship in public affairs as a town councillor. There was only one drawback to such a man, but it was substantial. He had no hope of winning.

The choice of Edgar Wallace, who did not obviously fit these specifications, was thus an imaginative gesture and an act of both faith and desperation.

Blackpool people at large were intrigued and flattered that their favour should be courted by a man like Wallace who, they believed, spent all hours of the day and most of the night writing stunning yarns at top speed, who earned vast quantities of *brass* and was known to everybody everywhere.

The unique profile, the long cigarette holder, the yellow Rolls: these became overnight the ikons of a cult. The legends spread; above all, of an unruffled, soft-spoken hero in silk dressing gown who, in the most luxurious suite of the Hotel Metropole, dictated campaign literature out of one corner of his mouth and novels out of the other.

Blackpool was thus only too happy to pose for the world press as Edgar Wallace's great and good friend. There were excellent pickings to be had in the way of publicity — on both sides, self-respect suggested — and the pulse beat excitingly faster at the thought of the reflected glory from such a suitor.

But as for a political marriage settlement, signed and sealed, that was something else. The Blackpool voter, like most others around the country, wanted a man (literally, for most of the women, and all of Labour's were defeated) who would fall in behind Stanley Baldwin and Ramsay MacDonald, and do what they told him. When they told him to die for the Gold Standard, he would salute and prepare to obey; when they told him to wring the Gold Standard's neck, he would feel no qualms.

The Liberals backed the National Government: all, that is, but Lloyd George, who was ill and out of the battle, and Edgar Wallace, who carried his own free lance. The Blackpool voter shook his head. Wallace might be a great hand at a crime novel, but who was he to know better than his betters about economic problems—than Baldwin, MacDonald, Herbert Samuel, and their devoted follower

C.C.A.L. Erskine-Bolst, FRGS?

The Blackpool voter turned up in symbolic numbers at meetings in lugubrious church halls and asked the Independent Liberal candidate what he proposed to do to put King Cotton back on his throne. The Independent Liberal candidate modestly said it was a subject he would need to examine more closely. The Blackpool voter, a last-ditch Free Trader only eight years earlier, decided there was no place for an MP who was not pledged to defend Lancashire from the imports of the underpaid, underhand foreigners.

Along the grapevine, if that is the right word, flashed the rumour that the speakers' water carafe at Wallace meetings was filled with champagne. The image projected, of a Baudelairean **luxe, calme et volupté**, seemed deliberately intended as a comment, oblique but unflattering, on the temperate rigours of board-residence in Blackpool.

Politically, the game was up. By three to one, the Blackpool voters confirmed their old allegiance. But as a faithful wife may be permitted to warm her memory at an old flame, so Blackpool now and then looks back, with a frisson of complacency, to the time, the only time, that a romantic figure of worldwide fame sought her hand.

After all, as the station bookstall girl was saying to me only this morning: "There's been no one like him, has there?"

BLACKPOOL FIRE BRIGADE   by Laurie Heaton

The earliest records of a fire brigade in Blackpool go back to 1858 when a manual pump was purchased by public subscription for the volunteer firemen.

In 1876 the newly formed Blackpool Borough Council created the *Fire Brigade and Watch Committee*. In 1877 Councillor George Bonny became the Honorary Superintendent and later the brigade's first full-time Superintendent.

In 1878 a fire station was built in the Corporation yard in Hull Street which is now part of the Hounds Hill Shopping Precinct. This station contained a horse-drawn steamer and a horse-drawn manual pump.

In 1888 control of the brigade was taken over by the Blackpool Borough Police and Inspector H. Sharrock was appointed Superintendent in charge with Mr T. Hall as his deputy. Policemen were appointed members of the brigade for which they received extra money but were on almost continuous duty. They became known as *fire-bobbies*.

The foundation stone for a new station was laid by Alderman James Fish JP who was Chairman of the Watch Committee on 26 October 1900 and the station was opened in 1901. The station, which is situated in Albert Road was next to the Police Headquarters in South King Street and consisted of three engine bays with stables for the horses. It was considered to be superbly equipped, having accommodation at the rear and in Charnley Road for firemen and their families.

In 1903 a Gamewell street fire alarm system was installed. It was only the second in the country.

In 1914 when the Chief Constable was Mr W.J. Pringle, the brigade consisted of only Police/firemen.

The first motor fire engine was purchased in 1913 and the second one in 1918 when horses were then dispensed with. In the 1930's, due to the continued growth of Blackpool, the work of both the police and the fire brigade had increased, so in 1935, in the interests of efficiency, it was decided to separate these two public services. Mr T.A. Varley came to Blackpool from St Helens on his appointment as Chief Fire Officer. The strength of the brigade at that time was thirty-six and it was equipped with the latest Leyland appliances.

With the threat of World War II the Auxiliary Fire Service was established to boost the strength of the service in the event of air raids. These volunteers were trained in

51

The Brigade outside the Fire Station in Hill Road, probably around the
time it opened in 1878

basic fire-fighting skills which proved to be invaluable when, in the early part of the war, large cities were bombed and destroyed by fire.

Two extra stations were opened in Blackpool, one in Red Bank Road, Bispham and the other in Lytham Road at the corner of Dean Street. There were also sub-stations throughout the town strategically placed to enable efficient fire cover for the whole town in the event of an air-raid and to give a back-up to other areas if necessary.

In 1941 the Government took over control of the fire brigades of the United Kingdom and formed the National Fire Service which continued until 1948. This control enabled the government to standardise the service so that all brigades, for the first time, had standard equipment, drill and uniforms. Before 1941 it was possible for neighbouring fire brigades to attend the same fire and not be able to combine the use of their hosepipes and pumps due to the different types being used.

On 1st April 1948 the brigades of the United Kingdom were returned to the control of local authorities and their strength reduced to a peace-time level. War-time grey appliances were re-painted red and radio communication became standard equipment.

In 1947 Mr E.H. Harmer MBE GM was appointed Chief Officer of the Blackpool County Borough Fire Brigade which now had three stations manned by full-time firemen. These stations contained three pump escapes, two turntable ladders, one pump salvage tender and one emergency tender. In 1963 the North fire station was rebuilt on the site of the old one in Red Bank Road and in 1973 the new South fire station was built in St Annes Road.

Mr Harmer retired in 1969 when Mr Len Smith, who had been the Deputy Chief, became Chief Officer.

On 1st April 1974 due to local government reorgan- isation, Blackpool, along with Lancashire, Preston, Blackburn and Burnley amalgamated to become the new Lancashire County Fire Brigade. Blackpool Central in Albert Road became the new 'B' Divisional Headquarters.

It would be wrong, when writing a potted history, to omit references to milestones which are referred to whenever firemen meet and talk with pride about the Blackpool Brigade.

In 1936, the Boots' Store on Market Street was gutted and occupied many hours of work for the Brigade. One of their number, young Raymond Laycock, perished whilst tackling the fire. Layton's Laycock Gate is named in his memory. In 1956, when the Tower Ballroom became an inferno, the Brigade pitted themselves against it, just as they did at the big fires over the years at the Pleasure Beach, Hill's Store, North Pier and the Imperial Cinema on Dickson Road.

★   ★   ★   ★   ★

FUEL FOR THOUGHT

Coal gas for domestic use was first introduced to Blackpool in 1852 under the provisions of the Blackpool Improvement Act of 1851. Its manufacture and sale were under the control of the Local Board, forerunner of the Corporation. The service was privately run between 1862 and 1869, when the Local Board again took over the running. In 1869 the total income of the Undertaking was £610, and the expenditure £58, giving a gross profit of £552, which was reduced to a net profit of £38 after loan charges were repaid. This magnificent sum was applied to the town's rates. In later years, when profits were much higher, profits were applied to various Corporation schemes, such as buying land, illuminations, decorations and pictures for the Art Gallery. This policy was reversed when the Undertaking objected to subsidising other departments and not being able to build up their Reserve Fund.

One of the factors which necessitated the buying of land at Marton to replace the original Princess Street Gas Works was that the Reserve Fund was low, and the sale of the valuable town-centre site would help toward the costs of the new one.

The Princess Street site occupied 11 acres, whereas the farm estate at Marton bought to replace it, occupied 100 acres, and was bought in the 1930's for £130 an acre.

In 1939, the Undertaking estimated the average daily demand for gas at 6 million cubic feet. In 1987, that average is 40 million cubic feet. Although this appears to be a 6.6 times increase, when the difference in heating capability between Coal gas and Natural gas is taken into account, it is nearer to 13 times more.

In 1939, 180 Blackpool chip shops used gas-fired ranges, resulting in a 10 p.m. peak of consumption each day during the holiday season. August was the peak supply month, and figures for the 1922, 1932 and 1939 seasons showed how the Illuminations, introduced in 1925 affected October sales.

54

The Marton gas works became operational in 1940, having been delayed a short time by the outbreak of war. Some of the costs of the new works were:-

New access road and drainage	£8,400
Works gate	£250
Building boundary wall and fence	£1,500
L.M.S. Railway sidings	£8,076
Works railway sidings	£16,996
Carbonizing plant & Coke plant	£199,075
Works locomotive	£1,590
Total costs	£366,681

The present record of daily consumption of gas supplied from Marton is 65 million cubic feet, reached in January 1987 during a very cold spell.

THE BLACKPOOL CO-OPERATIVE SOCIETY
by Joan Greenhalgh

No story or account of Blackpool would be complete or worthy of its salt without a mention of the Co-operative Society, which came to Blackpool in July 1885 in a shop in Lytham Street (now Corporation Street). It had very humble beginnings. 44 years later it had numerous shops and the Emporium situated in Coronation Street, which at one stage boasted three floors, offices, bank, basement, restaurant, and the Jubilee Theatre, capable of holding 500 people, which hosted many local events such as musicals, plays and dances.

Children were not forgotten and the Co-op Children's Fancy Dress Balls held a the Tower and Winter Gardens were memorable events for us 'Young Sand-Grown-un's'. Then there was the *Divi* which was paid twice a year. Just into the New Year came the Peter and Pam Painting Book which was distributed from the local branches to all members' children, with a prize for the best entry in the competition.

The first Co-operative Bakery was opened in Charnley Road in 1894 and in 1936 a new one was opened in Preston New Road, and Co-op bread vans selling pies, cakes and bread became familiar sights in all parts of the town.

The Co-op also had a dairy in George Street, which opened in 1930 and sold an average of 17,500 gallons of milk — 265,500 bottles — per week. Two years later the Meat Factory opened and by 1935 the Co-operative Society was the biggest meat purveyor in this part of the country. Amongst other Departments were those specialising in Coal, Undertaking, Travel, Photography, Pharmacy, Dentistry and Hairdressing.

There was even a mixed choir, founded in 1915. The Co-op Social Club for employees and associate members started in Victory Road and today is situated on Preston New Road, just past the old Co-op Bakery (which is now owned by the Gazette). The club consists of a large ballroom, lounge, and games room and on the outside are football pitches, playing fields and two bowling greens. For women there was, and still is, the Co-operative Women's Guild, which set out to educate working women and in the Edwardian era was often their only social outlet. The Co-op was indeed a way of life!

In October, 1935 the foundation stones of the new £100,000 extension to Blackpool's Co-operative Society's buildings in Coronation Street/Albert Road were laid by the surviving members of the original Board of Management, who included Mr John Leach of Hamilton, Ontario, who crossed the Atlantic at 78 years of age for the ceremony, which also marked the Golden Jubilee of the Society.

In 1985 the Co-operative Emporium in Coronation Street held an 'Olde Worlde Shoppe' to celebrate the 100 years and to coincide with the local festival week. Old fittings, shelving and counters were featured, with many original packages and tins from yesteryears. It created tremendous interest and evoked memories of old shops with their tub butter, sacks of flour and the wonderful smell of coffee beans. The ever changing pattern of shopping and today's needs are somewhat different and to accommodate these a large hypermarket, situated at Marton and employing 250 people serves the shopper of today, with everything under one roof.

On Saturday, June 15th, 1929 the Co-operative Education Committee held a Grand Gala and Children's Sports in Stanley Park. The admission was 6 pence (2½p) for adults, children half price. Each child attending was presented with a souvenir pot and supplied with milk and a bun.

Several local bands performed and the entertainment

also included Punch and Judy, a troupe of comedians, a gymnastic display, a ventriloquist and a final firework display. Could Mr John Leach have envisaged all this when he stood up in the Porters Room at Central Station over a century ago and pleaded with fellow workers to consider the possibility of setting up a workers' Co-op? He canvassed after the meeting and got 24 names, but alas 21 of the interested parties withdrew their names on the threat of loss of jobs if their interest in that business prevailed. One stalwart stood fast, a Mr Fred Watson. Between them they shared the cost of the hire of Clarke's Coffee Palace—1s 6d (7½p). This meeting had been advertised in the Blackpool Times on March 11th, 1885 for intending Co-operators. The attendance was very small, but a committee was formed and it was resolved to form 'The Blackpool Industrial Co-op Society Limited'. Their first meeting was held at the home of Mr Leach and the second took place on April 2nd, 1885, again at Clarke's Coffee Palace and the historic resolution was moved. The first quarterly meeting was held in September of the same year. Assets and liabilities both totalled £174 12s 0½d.

From such small beginnings grew the Blackpool Co-operative Society whose story is indeed one of the romances of Big Business—a precious heritage left to us by the single mindedness of those early pioneers.

ALONG THE RIGHT LINES:
BLACKPOOL—TRAMENDOUSLY PROGRESSIVE

by Peter Jackson

Blackpool, in the latter half of the Victorian age, was in many ways a thriving resort town. The railways, which had first reached the town proper in 1846, brought in visitors by the thousand from the grim industrial towns of Northern England and even further afield. They were eager for a sight of the sea and the beach, as well as eager to spend money on the many delights that Blackpool offered. The problem was—having alighted from the train at Talbot Road or Central Station, how was the visitor to make his way to the various parts of the town?

Prior to 1885, the usual means of transport was *Shanks' Pony*. True, there were a large number of horse-drawn landaus available for hire as well as some horse-drawn omnibuses which plied mainly on the Promenade. These landaus however were fairly expensive, and to increase the number of horse-drawn 'buses was not the straight-forward solution to the problem it might appear. Even for a town with a topography as hill-free as Blackpool, the use of horse-power brings with it many difficulties. The number of horses required is very large—each vehicle needing more than 8 animals during the course of a day. These horses must all be fed, looked after and stabled. It was clear to the town council that the solution to their problem did not lie in that direction, and it is to their credit that they adopted a then revolutionary form of transport for the town—the electric tramway.

The uses and potential applications of electricity were only just beginning to be realised during the late 19th century. True, Blackpool had, in 1879, been the first town in the country to introduce street lighting to a Promenade, but to use electricity to power a passenger-carrying tramcar was an entirely different matter. In 1884 however, one Michael Holroyd Smith had built a narrow gauge railway in the grounds of the Winter Gardens and that was powered by electricity. Volks Electric Railway had run at Brighton successfully, and the Giants' Causeway Tram-way in Northern Ireland was electric powered. Apart from these however, there was precious little evidence to prove that an electric tramway was a real possibility. But, true to the progressive spirit that was reflected in the various elements of Victorian Blackpool, the Town Council firmly grasped the nettle—an electric tramway would be built.

The momentous event occurred on 29th September 1885 when Blackpool's electric street tramway (the first of its kind in the world) was opened. It was celebrated in real style, with the whole town in festive mood, and civic dignitaries from all over North West England gathered to witness the new miracle. For the first time, mass urban transport was a very real possibility. More than that. It was fact.

The rest of the world was not slow to imitate Blackpool's success.

The tramway itself was a fairly small concern to start with, and many problems concerning its operation were to be encountered in the months and years ahead. The Town Council persevered, and Blackpool's tramways were to become second to none. The original line ran for a distance of nearly two miles along the promenade between Dean Street, near South Pier, and Cocker Street, towards the Northern end of the town. The electric current was obtained not from the overhead wires but from a channel between the running rails, known as *the conduit*. This conduit was a source of much anxiety to the tramway operators, for all too easily it became blocked by sand or affected by salt water driven across the track by the fierce gales that afflict Blackpool. In either instance of course, the electric current was short circuited and the whole operation came to a halt. Often during those early days, horses were brought in to trundle the electric tramcars up and down the promenade. But the potential of electric operation had been proved. Progress was inevitable. Furthermore, for the first time in any resort in the land, the visitor could travel at reasonable speed in reasonable comfort, and for a reasonable price, from almost one end of the town to the other.

During the following decade, debate raged fiercely as to how the tramway could be improved, and also as to how (or if) it was to be expanded. Eventually, in 1899, the Corporation adopted the principle of overhead current collection which endures to this day. Many additions were to be made to that original two-miles route, laying the foundations of a network of electric tramway covering most of Blackpool itself and providing connections to neighbours Fleetwood and Lytham St. Annes.

The first major extension came in 1895 when track was laid in Lytham Road so that contact could be made with the tramways of Lytham St. Annes (where the early cars were gas-powered). Two years later this route was joined again to the original promenade conduit system by the laying of tracks down Station Road. In 1898 the Blackpool and Fleetwood Tramroad Company commenced operations. That route ran from Talbot Road Railway Station along Dickson Road to The Gynn, then along the cliff to Bispham, Norbreck and Cleveleys, there to turn inland to eventually run into the town of Fleetwood. This was a private venture, financed privately and run for the twenty years or so of its life independently of the Corporation. Incidentally, the Company's successful use of overhead wire current collection from the commencement of their operations was a major factor influencing Blackpool's decision to convert to it. The tracks of the Corporation's own tramway were extended from the original Cocker Street terminus to the Gynn, where they met up with the new company's tracks. Thus, before Queen Victoria's reign drew to a close, it was possible to travel by tram (changing cars at times) from Fleetwood to Lytham St. Annes, a distance of more than 14 miles.

59

During this time, the Corporation were not slow to see the possibilities of extending the tramways to cover inland Blackpool as well as that strip of the town bordered by the Irish Sea. In 1901 the Marton route was inaugurated, running from Talbot Square to the Royal Oak, or even South Pier by way of Church Street, Whitegate Drive, the Oxford and Waterloo Road. In the same year, the Marton route was joined at the junction of Middle Lane (where St. Annes Road crosses Waterloo Road) by a route originating at Central Station and then running along Central Drive. In 1902, the Layton route was opened, running from Talbot Square as far as the cemetery. The final major tramway extension took place in 1926, several years after some municipalities had abandoned their tramways. This was along the new South Promenade as far as Starr Gate. The tramway map of Blackpool was finally complete.

The impact of the tramway on both visitor and local was profound. The former now enjoyed reliable transport to most parts of the town. Arriving at either of the major railway stations, the visitor had merely to walk a few yards to the nearest tram-stop. In a matter of minutes he would alight near his hotel or boarding house, thus being spared a long walk encumbered with the family's luggage. Hotels and boarding houses began to spread throughout the town. Previously the prime areas had been situated in the somewhat mean streets near to the rail terminals in order to attract custom. Thanks to the tramway network, this was no longer necessary. Hotels began to emerge in the more salubrious areas North and South of the town centre, sure in the knowledge that their guests would arrive safely and quickly by tram, and that in fact they would profit by being somewhat removed from the congested centre.

In the South of the town, the fair at the Pleasure Beach (for thus it was officially named in 1906) benefited greatly from its accessibility to the public. Other attractions too followed the steel tracks to lure the visitors, and separate him from part of his money. To the North, Fleetwood prospered from day-trippers conveyed there cheaply and swiftly on the single-decked cars of the Tramroad Company. Fleetwood Market became, and still is today, a major attraction to the visitor.

Local people found great advantages in the tramway system. At the time of its opening, the Marton route ran through almost rural surroundings. This was soon to change. Houses were built by the more affluent inhabitants near the route of the tramway. Thus they could live away from the hustle and bustle of central Blackpool, yet be at their place of work in a matter of minutes. Where there are houses, there is a need for shops, and so it proved in Marton. Then, of course, schools and all the other services demanded by a growing community. Exactly the same phenomenon occurred along the route to Fleetwood. The small villages of Bispham, Norbreck and Cleveleys soon developed into thriving communities, secure in their ease of access to the generation of wealth — Blackpool.

The pace of progress and development continued unabated during the early years of the 20th Century. To explain development is often to confront the *chicken and egg* situation, in which it is not possible to state which came first. In the case of Blackpool tramways, this is not so. The steel tracks came first, and people, never slow to grasp an opportunity, followed. The tramways played a vital role in the history of Blackpool.

Blackpool Tram Depot (Marton) Whitegate Drive c. 1927. Mr Ayrton (conductor) third from left, back row. Given by Mr Ayrton.

A DOUBLE CAUSE FOR CELEBRATION
From *The Graphic* 10th October, 1885

The new lifeboat and electric tramway at Blackpool

FETE AT BLACKPOOL

An interesting celebration took place on Tuesday, September 29th at Blackpool, that favourite Lancashire watering-place. The main features of the programme were the launching of a lifeboat, and the opening of an electric tramway.

The lifeboat came into existence this way. A Manchester pawnbroker named Samuel Fletcher died intestate, and his estate reverted to the Crown. But as, before his death, he had expressed a wish to endow a lifeboat, a sum sufficient for that purpose was ordered by Her Majesty to be placed at the disposal of the Royal National Lifeboat Institution, and a first-class lifeboat was built. This was sent to the Blackpool station, where it displaces the *Robert Williams,* which, during its twenty-one years of service on the coast has been instrumental in saving a very large number of lives.

The Electric Street Tramway is two miles long, and extends along the whole length of the foreshore promenade. It has been constructed according to the plans of Mr Holroyd Smith, electrical engineer. By his system an underground channel is placed in the centre of the track. Its surface consists of street troughing filled with wooden paving blocks, and forms a roadway. The sides of the channel are partially formed of creosoted wood, holding porcelain insulators, which carry electric conductors.

The positive electricity passes along these conductors, the return is made by means of the rails, which are electrically connected one with the other. To generate the electricity, a prime mover drives a dynamo, and these dynamos are so made that they produce just the amount of electric energy required, and no more. The generators fixed at the Blackpool engine-shed are capable of driving ten loaded cars — sufficient to carry 400 passengers.

The day of the celebration was remarkably fine. The procession included various local bodies, and the Mayors and Mayoresses of a number of Lancashire, Yorkshire and other adjacent towns. The tramway was opened by Alderman R. Horsfall of Halifax. Instructed by Mr Holroyd Smith, he set the electric current in motion, and caused the car to move a few yards forward.

Then followed the launching of the lifeboats, which proved a very interesting spectacle. These boats were the Lytham and St. Annes boats, the *Robert Williams* (the old Blackpool lifeboat) and the *Samuel Fletcher,* the new boat, which was formally presented by Lieut. Tipping, on behalf of the Queen. The Mayor of Liverpool, before breaking the bottle of wine over the new boat's bows, referred to the history and work of the National Life Boat Institution. Last year, eighteen vessels were saved and 633 persons rescued from drowning by the aid of the Society's boats. The *Samuel Fletcher*, which floated the Royal Standard, was then released from the hulks, and glided gracefully into the water.

The procession was then re-formed, and, preceded by a train driven by the Mayor of Manchester, returned to Talbot Square. Later in the afternoon the Mayor of Blackpool entertained a number of guests in the Borough Hall, and in the evening the town was illuminated, and there was a display of fireworks from the piers.

THE EARLY METHODISTS

The earliest Blackpool Methodists were people from the Fylde villages who came to Blackpool to preach the Gospels to the early visitors. The first Fylde Methodist was Betty Tomlinson, whose husband had been transformed by the Gospels from wife-beating brute to zealous worker for Christ. The most prominent however was William Bramwell, born in an Elswick cottage in 1759. He was concerned with the building of the first chapel at Thornton in 1812, and that at Poulton in 1819.

In 1830, after years in which Methodism had waned and flourished, James Roskell, who was associated with those chapels, gathered some friends together after coming to live in Little Layton. He and Robert Bird, a draper with a shop near where the Tower stands today, encouraged friends to meet in Bonny's Bathing House, near to the present-day Central Pier. Two years later, at Garstang, it was resolved "that Blackpool should be tried once a month as a preaching place". They met on a Sunday evening at six o'clock in the Bathing House, then in Bird's Bazaar when it became too small. This too soon proved inadequate, and it was decided to provide a suitable chapel. It was opened in 1835 where the Hounds Hill Centre is now, and where until the 1970's the Methodist Chapel stood. Remember, in 1835 the railway hadn't reached Blackpool, and the population of the town was about 2,000. In 1846, the railway arrived, and by 1861 the population was 3,506. It was this population boom and the zeal of the Blackpool Methodists that brought about the replacement, in 1862, of the first chapel by that which was demolished in the late 1970's to make way for the Hounds Hill Centre, included in which is the present-day Central Methodist Chapel.

A short time after the chapel was built, a schoolroom was added, and in 1910 the chapel was enlarged. However, the town needed yet more chapels, and others were built in Dickson Road (£7,000) and Raikes Parade (£6,500) before the First World War.

THE GOLDEN AGE OF THE GOLDEN MILE

by Ellis Clark

My earliest recollection of the Golden Mile was watching the carnivals of 1923/24 and seeing my uncle selling pigs' bladders which had been blown up to the size of a balloon and attached to a stick by a piece of string. These were sold to crowds of holidaymakers who continued their walk along the Prom hitting all and sundry with the bladders.

The Golden era of the Mile began when Luke Gannon appeared on the scene in the late 1920's. I first remember him doing a mind reading act with a lovely young lady billed as Madame Kusharny on a piece of land known as "No Man's Land", on which now stands the Lion Hotel. It received its name from the fact that nobody would trace the owner, so, consequently, people could set up their wares without paying rent. Luke's next involvement on the Mile was when he exhibited a starving man in a glass case. He fasted on liquids only for sixty days. This man was a local character named "Bandy" because of his bow legs. His money had to be brought to him each day by the doctor, who entered the case to examine him, then left and the sealing tapes were re-sealed and signed by the public. This was to stop any secret feeding. This venture didn't look as if it would prove successful at first, but as time went by people who had been for a day at Whit returned for their annual holiday, saw that he was still fasting, and flocked in to see him at 2d a time. During the last few days of his fast, there was a continual queue. The following year, Luke had another man fasting. He was known as "The Great Sacco". These two were the forerunners of a spate of fasting men at other resorts throughout the country. The following year, the pitch moved to the corner of Brunswick Street, near to where Ripley's "Believe it or not" exhibition was in the 1970's. There Luke exhibited a starving bride called Joyce Heather, who, immediately after marrying, entered a huge barrel with a glass window inserted so that the public could view her fasting. She had to go without food or water for ten days and if she was able to complete the task, she was to receive £200, a princely sum then. Joyce gave up on the ninth day, and the public didn't care for this, saying that she had been made to give up so that Luke would not have to pay out. Knowing Luke Gannon though, I doubt if she suffered financially. The public protest lead to a confrontation on the forecourt of the show. The crowd rolled the barrel across the prom and into the sea. Traffic was stopped for ages. The daily newspapers made the story headlines the next day, and this made Luke famous. His attitude was that of the well known show business adage—"I don't care what they say so long as they spell my name right."

Next season, the barrel was used to exhibit another much publicised figure—"The Rector of Stiffkey" who had been unfrocked by the Church for his associations with prostitutes. This time the barrel had the front cut away entirely so that people could converse or shake hands with him, which they did in great numbers. Amusingly, the public could have seen him free of charge, because at meal times he would don his black Homburg hat, light a cigar and saunter off to the nearest hotel to partake of his favourite beverage. Sadly, he met an untimely death at another resort after being mauled by a lion.

As a teenager, I was employed as a "gee", which is a young person who pretends to be a patron of the game concerned in order to attract more players. As people begin to congregate, the gee melts into the background to wait until the next time a pitch was needed. The game was a racing game for 12 players, who each had an electric button in front of them with the name of a well known race horse painted on it. These corresponded with a panel of names above the stall which lit up the names of the horses as a small replica of a horse passed along the perimeter of the stall. On the command "All Press", each player had to press the button, and wherever the horse stopped, that player would receive a prize.

Continuing the Luke Gannon story .... He once sent a 26 years old woman midget to Claremont Infant School all one winter, posing as a 10 years old. Just before the season started, the truth was leaked out and the Education Authorities expelled her. She was then exhibited in his show under the sign "See the girl who hoaxed the Education Committee." Newspaper headlines of that nature ensured another successful venture.

There were many sideshows. At one, a group of giraffe-necked African women were exhibited. They wore brass rings around their necks, which stretched to an enormous length. Then there was a tribe of Africans who had small discs or plates inside their lips, which protruded a great distance from their faces. These were billed "The Plate-lipped Savages from Darkest Africa". There too as Jolly, the fattest woman in the world, and Mary Ann Bevan, the ugliest woman in the world. Andy, the lobster-clawed man who had no arms, just two small hands protruding from his shoulders. He could perform great feats of juggling and balancing with them. There was a bearded lady, a troupe of midgets and many, many others.

The Sands between Central Pier and Woolworths were very colourful then. Besides the Punch and Judy shows there were two different ventriloquists who used to perform on very high stepladders with a seat on. There was Frank Dennis, a magician, who did sleight-of-hand and balancing tricks. On Central Pier a man was bound up in a sack, which was then set alight before he dived into the sea, emerging unscathed, to the delight of the crowd which had gathered. Another feature of the beach was the long rows of bathing huts on wheels. They were driven back and forth by large horses as the tide receded. People were allowed to sell rock on the sands when the tide had gone out past a point on the pier, so there was a cavalcade of horses and carts belonging to various rock makers, all making a dash to be the first to set up their pitch and draw a crowd, which they did by throwing free rock. Local children knew the drill and were always at the front of the crowd as each trader set up his pitch.

Then there were the song-booths, where holidaymakers were able to sing the popular songs of the day, and buy sheet music and song-books with the words and music in. One of the demonstrators was George Mee, a Blackpool and England footballer who became licensee of the Shakespeare Hotel on Topping Street. One of the publishing firms was Lawrence Wright's, who were very publicity-conscious. One season he hired Jack Hylton's band to fly over Central Beach in an aeroplane playing one of his songs, "Me and Jane in a plane", through amplifiers to the crowd below.

REFLECTIONS ON
BLACKPOOL BOROUGH POLICE FORCE
by D.E. Heaney

This essay was written in 1969 to commemorate the amalgamation of the Blackpool Borough Police with the
Lancashire Constabulary. It has been up-dated only
slightly.

CHIEF CONSTABLES
J. C. Derham, Esq., 1887-1911
W. J. Pringle, Esq., 1911-1919
H. E. Derham, Esq., 1919-1935
E. H. Holmes, Esq., 1936-1942
H. Barnes, Esq., 1942-1958
H. E. Sanders, Esq., 1958-1962
S. Parr, Esq., 1962-1967
A. Rydeheard, Esq., 1967-1969

By a remarkable coincidence the new Police Headquarters for Blackpool, which had been planned to take
the place of the now inadequate and out-of-date Police
Station in South King Street, is sited near to the spot where
Blackpool's first Police Station stood. On 1st April, 1969,
the Blackpool County Borough Police Force was amalgamated with the Lancashire Constabulary, from which it
sprang.

In its early days, Blackpool Police administration came
under the jurisdiction of the County Magistrates, and
before the County Magistrates began to hold courts in
Blackpool, those who broke the law were dealt with at
Poulton. The County Court was also there until its removal
in the 1880's.

For about five hundred years, the Court of Petty
Sessions was held in the old courthouse at Poulton, the
ancient *capital of the Fylde*. In the early part of the 17th
century Quarter Sessions were also held there. The courthouse stood in Hardhorn Road, near to Sheaf Street, but
it has now disappeared.

After the middle of the last century, there was only one
policeman in Blackpool to keep the peace among both
residents and visitors. This officer was called Banks and
the Police Station was in Bonny Street.

The Quarter Sessions made an Order in April, 1853,
that a Police Station was to be provided. Following this,
seven Justices of the Peace in the Kirkham Division
negotiated with John Bonny, a Blackpool merchant, for the
purchase of a plot of land, an area of some 260 square
yards on the east side of Bonny Street, at a price of £39.

On 1st June, 1853, the land was conveyed to the seven Justices for the purpose of erecting the Police Station.

The first Police Station was a small building, as can be imagined from the area of the land on which it was built, and in 1862 a new Station was built in Abingdon Street. Even today there is *Police Street*, at the rear of the Post Office in Abingdon Street. The money received from the sale of the old Station defrayed the cost of the new building.

An interesting anecdote concerns a historian of Blackpool, the Reverend William Thornber. In his later years, shortly before a Police Force was established in the town, Mr Thornber showed signs of mental disturbance. An order for his detention was sent to the Police department, and Sergeant Whiteside was detailed to arrest the gentleman, whom he found in Talbot Road, near to some excavations for the laying of sewers. The Sergeant said, "Hey, I want to see you". "Oh, do you?", replied the ex-vicar, striking the officer a blow which left him lying on his back in the excavations.

On 21st January, 1876, Blackpool received its Charter of Incorporation and became a Borough. Eleven years later, in 1887, the Blackpool Borough Police Force was formed and the Quarter Sessions ceased to have control of the Police. At the census in 1881, the population of the Borough was 14,229 and was estimated at the formation of the Borough Force to be about 20,000.

Mr John Christopher Derham, at the age of 40 years, was appointed as the first Chief Constable, on 3rd June, 1887, and within three weeks he had increased the size of the Force to one Chief Constable, three Sergeants, and 16 Constables, a total of 20 men. On 10th September, 1887, the establishment was increased by one Constable. The names of the members of the original Force were, Chief Constable John Christopher Derham, Sergeants William Pethybridge, John William Farmery, and Robert Davies, Constables James Baldwin, George Wycherley, Arthur Squires, Joseph Hanks, Thomas Farrow, Thomas Kieling, William Lambert, William Milne, John Robert Becconsall, John Moore, Richard Parkinson, Albert Jenkinson, William Collier, Sergeant Kendall, Ebenezer Swindlehurst, Frank Hockney, and William Hay Lawrence.

The salary of the Chief Constable was £200 per year, a sergeant was paid 31/- per week, a senior constable 25/2d., and a junior constable 24/-.

Mr Derham was the son of a police officer and had

served in the County Force since 1870. Soon after joining the Service he was sent, as P.C. Derham, as the Officer in Charge of the Marton area where he remained for 18 months. The rest of his service in the County was spent at Kirkham where he reached the rank of Sergeant.

Mr Derham remained as Blackpool's Chief Constable until his death in 1911. He is buried in Layton Cemetery where his bust looks out over Annesley Avenue. His funeral ceremony is said to have been the biggest held in the town up to that time.

Mr Derham is particularly remembered for his work with the St. John's Ambulance Brigade. In fact, he founded the Brigade in the town. He also founded the Poor Children's Clothing Fund and rendered invaluable help to Victoria Hospital after its opening in Whitegate Drive during the 1890's.

On his 60th birthday, in 1907, Mr Derham was presented with an inscribed silver salver and a cheque for £500 by his many friends in the town. Members of the Police Force gave him an illuminated address and an album containing photographs of all members of the Force.

In 1891, the population of Blackpool was 23,846 and was increasing rapidly. The number of visitors steadily increased and the police buildings in Abingdon Street were found to be totally inadequate. On 5th June, 1895, the Headquarters in South King Street was opened by the then Mayor, Alderman James Cardwell. Councillor (later Alderman) James Fish, who was the Chairman of the Watch Committee, said that the former premises in Abingdon Street had been totally inadequate for the purposes of the Court, but they would, however, find the new building quite suitable, though not sumptuously adorned, but of a character which was eminently fitting for Blackpool.

The Mayor was presented with a gold key. He declared that the Police Station was a credit to Blackpool and to all who had anything to do with it.

Before the First World War, and for a number of years after it, the single policemen whose homes were outside the town lived in the police buildings. There are still some people who remember them creeping back to their quarters long after the off duty curfew hours, through a back entrance.

On 27th August, 1898, the Borough was granted its own Commission of the Peace. The original Bench had 23 Magistrates, of whom 10 served on the County Bench. The new Justices were sworn in by the Town Clerk on 7th

September that year and were afterwards entertained to lunch by the Mayor.

Mr W.J. Dickson was appointed as the Magistrates' Clerk. He had served as Clerk to the County Magistrates for nearly 30 years. He appointed Mr Hugh Singleton who had been with him for 27 years, as his deputy.

Mr Singleton later served as Magistrates' Clerk for years. His son, Mr E.H. Singleton, became a member of the Bench in 1956, and later was its Chairman.

On 1st October, 1904, Blackpool became a County Borough.

The Police Force continued to expand as the town grew and Police Stations were opened at Montague Street, Hawes Side Lane, and Talbot Road (then called New Road).

In 1911, following the death of Mr J.C. Derham, Mr W.J. Pringle was appointed Chief Constable. He was a fine figure of a man, a good horseman, and was Chief Constable throughout the whole of the First World War.

The most outstanding act of heroism by a Blackpool Police Officer during the war was that of Acting Inspector Alfred Victor Smith. Whilst serving as a Lieutenant in the East Lancashire Regiment at Gallipoli, he saved several of his fellow officers and men from certain death at the cost of his own life. He was in a trench when he dropped a grenade. Realising that the grenade would explode at any moment he threw himself on top of it and thereby saved his comrades. He was 24 years of age at the time and was posthumously awarded the last Victoria Cross of 1915.

Lieutenant Smith was born in Surrey and educated at Burnley Grammar School, and was the only son of the then Chief Constable of Burnley. His portrait hangs in the Towneley Museum, Burnley, and there is a plaque to his memory near to the Memorial Chapel in St John's Parish Church, Blackpool.

In 1917, the Urban District of Bispham-with-Norbreck and part of Carleton, were incorporated into the County Borough and a new Police Station was opened in a house which had been the offices of the Bispham-with-Norbreck Urban District Council.

Mr W.J. Pringle was succeeded by Mr H. E. Derham, the son of the first Chief Constable. He is said to have had a kind heart and a stentorian voice which could be heard all over the Headquarters—he needed no telephone to contact the various departments.

In 1927 the strength of the Force had risen to 118, and by 1934 it was 132.

Following Mr H.E. Derham the Chief Constables have been Mr E.H. Holmes, Mr H. Barnes, Mr. H.E. Sanders, Mr S. Parr, and Mr A. Rydeheard.

Mr Sanders retired in 1967 as an Assistant Chief Constable in the Lancashire Constabulary When he came to Blackpool in 1938 he was responsible for much modernisation and reorganisation of the Force.

This modernisation was consolidated by Mr Parr during his years as Chief Constable between 1962 and 1967. Mr Parr left Blackpool for his parent Force in 1967, and became Chief Constable of the Lancashire Constabulary.

Mr Rydeheard was Acting Chief Constable between the time that Mr Parr left and the amalgamation and he was responsible for further improvements in the Force, including the Unit Beat Policing system. Following the amalgamation, Mr Rydeheard continued as Chief Superintendent commanding the Police in Blackpool, together with the Fylde area in the new Blackpool Division with a strength of 560 men and women of all ranks.

Blackpool obtained its own Quarter Sessions and Recorder in 1948.

In its 82 years of the Blackpool Police Force, the population of the town increased from about 20,000 to 152,133. The latter figure was taken from the 1961 census.

The establishment of the Force rose from 20 to 356, as the volume of crime increased. Those 19 cases of larceny in 1893 were represented by 3,805 crimes in 1968.

1st April, 1969, the Blackpool County Borough Police Force returned as part of the Lancashire Constabulary.

Central Police Station, South King Street. Opened in 1895 and in use until 1974, this photo was probably taken around the turn of the century. It was on a postcard, addressed to Miss Lilian Derham (Chief Constable's daughter) at 31 South King Street, and may have been written by H.E. Derham (her brother?) who was to become Chief after the Great War.

THE BOROUGH POLICE IN 1887

Chief Constable: John C. Derham

Abingdon Street Police Station: Sergeants: W. Pethybridge and Robert Davies. Constables: George Wycherley, Arthur Squires, Thomas Keeling, William Lambert, John Moore, Richard Parkinson, Albert Jenkinson, William Collier, William Henry Lawrence, Michael Monaghan.

Montague Street Police Station: Sergeant John Farmery. Constables: James Baldwin, William Milne, S. Kendell, Eber Swindlehurst, Frank Hockney.

It was a common thing for newly-formed police forces to have no provision for a rank structure as we know it today. Hence, in the Blackpool Force, there were no Inspectors, nor a Deputy Chief Constable, initially. In the Lancashire County Force, there were no Sergeants when the Force was first started, in 1839.

Blackpool Borough Police - probably the whole force - outside Montague Street Police office about 1890. The uniform is very similar to that of the Lancashire County Force of that time.

SOME BOROUGH BYE-LAWS

Bye-Laws are made under the authority of a parent Act of Parliament by the Town Council. They are interesting to look at, as they reflect light on the social activities and problems of the times for which they were enacted.

Those relating to Shoe-blacks were made in 1880. They allowed for the granting, by the Corporation, of licences which would be issued at the General Annual Licensing Day (the first Monday in March) and would last a year. They could be evoked if a shoe-black was convicted of any offence against the bye-laws. He had to wear his badge on his breast, showing his particular number as registered. There were 11 places at which up to 3 shoe-blacks might stand, 9 of them being on the Promenade and 3 opposite the Railway Stations. The shoe-black could stand on one of them for one week, when he had to move to the next stand on the rota, standing there for a week, then moving on again, according to the rota. He was entitled to demand and take for the cleaning of each pair of boots, the magnificent sum of one penny, but if he offended against the bye-laws, he could be fined five pounds, and in the case of a continuing offence, a further penalty of two pounds for each day after the Corporation had given him written notice of the offence being committed.

The Blackpool Improvement Act of 1893 was the authority allowing the Corporation, in 1899, to make bye-laws relating to the use of Claremont Park and the approaches to it. No person could drive a carriage into the Park, nor could they distribute handbills or circulars, or importune anyone for the purpose of selling to them or obtaining their custom. Of course, they couldn't behave in a riotous or indecent manner either, nor be there for betting purposes, nor play football, quoits, bowls, hockey, cricket or other games, nor "exhibit any noisy or dangerous performance" (the mind boggles as to what was meant by that). The maximum fine for offenders was five pounds.

A person of the female sex shall not, while bathing, approach within fifty yards of any place at which any person of the male sex above the age of ten years, may be set down for the purpose of bathing, or at which any such person may bathe. (1879)

Every proprietor or attendant of a bathing machine so constructed as to be capable of being drawn to or moved from the station occupied by such machine on any stand, by means of a horse or windlass, or other animal or mechanical power, shall at all times when such machine may be hired or used by any person for the purpose of bathing, cause such machine to be drawn or moved into such a depth of water, or otherwise into such a position as will prevent any indecent exposure of any such person when set down from such machine for the purpose of bathing, or when bathing from such machine. (1879)

Every person of the male sex above the age of ten years who may hire or use any bathing machine for the purpose of bathing, or may be set down from such machine for such purpose, shall at all times while bathing, wear suitable drawers or other sufficient dress or covering to prevent indecent exposure of the person. (1879)

(females had to wear "a suitable gown or other sufficient dress to prevent indecent exposure of the person")

Every boatman or other person in charge of a pleasure boat or vessel shall conduct himself with civility and propriety towards every person hiring or seeking to hire such boat or vessel. (1879)

A person shall not beat or shake any carpet, drugget, mat, rug or fabric upon any part of the parade or place or lay any blanket, sheet, quilt, towel, bathing apparel, linen or article of clothing upon the parade within a distance of fifteen yards from the westerly side of the carriage drive, or upon any step, post, rail, stump or hulking, barrier pole, on or in the parade. (1887)

A person shall not preach or hold or conduct any religious service or deliver, recite or read aloud any extract or passage from a book or pamphlet, or any public speech, lecture, sermon or address of any kind or description, on any part of the parade. (1882)

A person shall not, without the express permission of the Corporation first had and obtained, erect, or suffer to be erected any booth, shed or erection on the foreshore. (1895)

A person shall not, upon any part of the foreshore, by calling out, or other wise, importune any person to purchase any article, or offer for sale any article, or ply for any bathing machine or pleasure boat to the annoyance of such person, or of any other person. (1895)

No person hawking, offering or exposing for sale or selling any goods, wares merchandise or thing in any street, or on the foreshore or sands within the Borough, shall, in the excercise of his calling, blow a horn or whistle, ring a bell, or use any noisy instrument, or to the annoyance of any resident or passenger, shout, sing, call or cry out. (1887)

Every person hawking, offering or exposing for sale, or

selling any goods, wares, merchandise, or thing and in the excercise of his calling shout, singing, calling or crying out any article for sale in any street or on the foreshore or sands within the Borough, shall, on being required so to do by any Police Constable, desist from further shouting, singing, calling or crying out any article for sale in such street, or on such foreshore or sands. (1887)

The occupier of any premises fronting, adjoining or abutting on any street, shall, as soon as conveniently may be after the cessation of any fall of snow, remove or cause to be removed from the footways and pavements adjoining such premises all snow fallen or accumulated on such footways and pavements in such a manner and with such precautions as will prevent any undue accumulation in any channel or carriageway or upon any paved crossing. (1879)

Every person who, for the purpose of facilitating the removal of any snow from any footway or pavement, shall throw salt upon such snow shall forthwith effectually remove from such footway or pavement the whole of the deposit resulting from the mixture of the salt with the snow. (1879)

The occupier of any premises shall not keep any swine or deposit any swine's dung within the distance of sixty feet from any dwelling-house, or in such a situation as to pollute any water supplied for use or used or likely to be used by man for drinking or domestic purposes or for manufacturing drinks for the use of man, or any water used or likely to be used in any dairy. (1879)

A person shall not construct an Advertising Van in such a manner as to provide on any part thereof a space which, being intended for the reception of advertisements, shall exceed seven feet in length, six feet in height (measuring from the ground) and four feet six inches in width. (1882)

A person shall not, in any public thoroughfare, tout for a hotel, lodging-house, pier, boat, garden or theatre. (1882)

A person shall not in any street, or market, or on the parade, or on the foreshore or sands, within the borough, sell, deliver or expose to any inhabitant or passenger any posting bill, paper, print, photograph, picture, representation, book or card (whether enclosed in a sealed envelope or not) of an obscene, indecent, or offensive nature or referring to any disease of a loathsome or secret kind. 1887)

Any person calling or sending for any Porter's Cart and not further employing the same, shall pay to the proprietor, driver, conductor or attendant thereof, the sum of sixpence (1880)

A driver of an ass shall not solicit or allow any person to mount such ass for the purpose of being carried for hire when such person may know or have reasonable grounds for believing that the condition of such ass is such as to expose its rider or any person traversing or being in any street or public thoroughfare, to risk of danger (1894)

No boy under the age of eleven years shall be employed in or carry on street trading (1906)

No girl under the age of fourteen years, unless accompanying and assisting a parent or guardian bona fide engaged in street trading, shall be employed in or carry on street trading (1906)

No child who is not exempt from school attendance shall be employed in or carry on street trading during school hours (1906)

Every keeper of a common lodging house shall cause all bed-clothes and bedding, and every bed-stead used in such house, to be thoroughly cleansed, from time to time, as often as shall be requisite for the purpose of keeping such bed-clothes, bedding and bed-stead in a clean and wholesome condition (1884)

A keeper of a common lodging-house shall not cause or suffer any bed in any room which may be used as a sleeping apartment by persons of the male sex above the age of ten years to be occupied at any one time by more than one such person (1884)

A person shall not smoke any tobacco in the market house (1879)

The proprietor of every Porter's Cart, whether drawn by hand, or by one or more horses, before the same shall ply for hire, shall cause the number of his licence to be painted in a conspicuous position on the outside thereof, in white figures of not less than one inch in height....(1880)

A person shall not, in any public thoroughfare, tout for a Hotel, Lodging-house, Pier, Boat, Garden or Theatre. (1882)

The driver of every car (i.e. any carriage using any tramway within the Borough) shall cause the same to be driven or propelled along the Tramways at a speed which shall not exceed the rate of eight miles an hour (1902)

The driver of every car (i.e. carriage using any tramway within the Borough) shall so drive the same that it shall not follow a preceding car at a less distance than twenty yards (1902)

A passenger (on a tramway car) not being an artisan, mechanic or daily labourer within the true meaning of the Acts of Parliament or provisional orders relating to the tramways and portions of tramways belonging to and worked by the Corporation shall not use or attempt to use any ticket or any special carriage intended only for such artisans, mechanics or daily labourers (1902)

TAXI

A look at cab fares at the turn of the century:-

(To or from Talbot Square):- Per hour 3s, every additional quarter hour 9d. Belle Vue 1s 6d; Central Station 1s; Central Pier 1s; Imperial Hotel 1s; Manchester Hotel 1s; Raikes Hall 1s; South Shore 2s; Talbot Road Station 1s; Uncle Tom's Cabin 1s 6d; Victoria Pier 2s. (These prices are for 1-horse carriages.)

The hackney carriage driver of those times was controlled by Bye Laws made by the Urban Sanitary Board in 1879. Under them, the driver could not smoke when driving without the hirer's permission. He could not feed the horse except by a proper bag suspended from the horse's head or with hay held in the feeder's hand. If he carried a dead body, he was obliged to notify the Inspector of Nuisances. He had to keep the carriage's lamps properly trimmed and ready for lighting, and light them when the public streets were required to be lighted. The Harness was to be kept in perfect order. The driver of an open omnibus could not stand or ply for hire before 6 a.m. or after 11 p.m. Neither could he or his conductor or any person travelling on or using that omnibus play upon any horn or other musical instrument, or ring any bell.

In the main, the regulations affecting the cabbie or yesteryear still apply to those driving the motorised or horse-drawn cab today.

BLACKPOOL'S PUBLIC HOUSES - 1886

Some notes extracted from the Report of Superintendent Stafford of the Kirkham Division to the Licensing Justices sitting at Blackpool in August 1886.

LICENSED VICTUALLERS:

Occupier	Sign	Owner
Ben Bowman	Red Lion, Bispham	Susey Dewhurst
Richard Bennett	Albion Hotel, Bispham	Richard Warbrick
Cornelius Cardwell	Uncle Tom's Cabin	David Ashworth
Joseph Harrison	South Shore Hotel, Spring Terrace	Ellen Riley
Thomas Eccles	Commercial Hotel, Waterloo Road	M. Brown & Co
Betsy Fair	Britannia Hotel, Britannia Place	Jenny Dixon
Peter Isherwood	Dog & Patridge	John Tattersall
John Brook	Royal Oak	Occupier
Leo Waddington	Albert Hotel	William Kay
Elizabeth Seedall	Old Bridge House Inn	Thomas Jackson
J. Ed. Porter	Manchester Hotel	Margaret Hemingway
Tom Lockwood	Foxhall Hotel	Exors of Richard Caton
James Eccles	Princess Hotel	Occupier
James N. Davies	Ardwick Hotel	Mary Jane Worthington
Jennett Halliwell	Prince of Wales Inn	James Taylor
John Bickerstaffe	Wellington Hotel	John Bickerstaffe
Lawson Whittaker	Victoria Hotel	John Bickerstaffe
Robert B. Mather	New Inn	Jane Kay
Richard E. Taylor	Clarence Hotel, Hounds Hill	John Clegg
Tom Partington	Palatine Hotel	Manchester Equitable Co-op Soc.
Sarah Rowan	Royal Hotel, Adelaide Street	Royal Hotel Co.
Ralph Rushton	Beach Hotel, Victoria St	Central Property Co
Michael Taylor	County & Lane Ends	Lane Ends Estate Co
John W. Mycock	Albion Hotel, Central Beach	Robert Nickson
Roger Thompson	Clifton Arms Hotel, Belle Vue Square	Clifton Arms Hotel Co
Charles Barker	Fleece Inn	Daniel Thwaites
William Kay	Castle Inn, Market St	Exors of Wm. Carr
Elizabeth Coupland	Crown Hotel, Lytham St.	Wm. Birch
John Milner	Market Hotel, Lytham St.	M. Brown & Co
Humphrey Nicholson	Adelphi Hotel, Church St	Geo. B. Taylor
John R. Hudleston	Winter Gardens	Winter Gardens Co
Robert Nickson	Station Hotel	Robert Nickson

Occupier	Sign	Owner
Frederick Nickson	Talbot Hotel	Robert Nickson
Albert Fisher	Railway Hotel	Lucy H. Fisher
Henry Harris	Imperial Restaurant Talbot Rd	Blackpool Assembly
Ellen Bailey	Bailey's Hotel, Warbreck Rd	Occupier
Wm. Noore	Derby Hotel Warbreck Rd	John Read
Joseph Downs	Duke of York Hotel	Henry Hall
Henry Webster	Claremont Hotel, Claremont Park	W.H. Cocker
Samuel Crewe	Imperial Hotel, Claremont Park	Imperial Hotel Co
Thomas Noblett	Duke of Cambridge, Gynn	M. Brown & Co
Archibald Hislop	Mount Pleasant Hotel	M. Brown & Co
James Swarbrick	King's Arms Hotel, New Road	Occupier
Florence Wilson	Washington Hotel	Robert Whiteside
John Irish	Veever's Hotel	Exors of John Noblett
Joseph Bleasdale	Raikes Hotel, Cookson Street	Exors of Geo. Ormerod
Wm. Pemberton	Queen's Hotel, New Road	Wm. Fisher
Betty Wilson	Mill Inn, Carleton Road	Ellen Bissett
John Ward	No 4 & Freemason's Tavern, Gt. Layton village	Lawrence Banks
Elizabeth Potts	No 3 & Didsbury Hotel	John Garside
Wm. Bamber	Raikes Hall Hotel	Raikes Hall Gardens Co
Mary Smith	Belle Vue Hotel Whitegate Lane	John Hodgson
Whittaker Bond	Stanley Arms, Church St	Occupier
Thomas Altham	Clifton Arms Hotel, Little Marton Village	Trustees of J.T. Clifton
Thomas Ferguson	Cherry Tree Hotel, Moss Side	Occupier
Ralph Braithwaite	Shovels Inn, Folds	Thomas Braithwaite
Andreŵ Fox	Saddle Inn, Gt Marton Village	Exors of Geo. Ormerod
John Jackson	Oxford Hotel, Marton Green	Occupier
Thomas Melling	Bay Horse Hotel, Lytham Rd	M. Brown & Co
John Pearson	Coffee House, Lytham Rd	Occupier

BEER & WINE "ON" LICENCES

Occupier	Sign	Owner
John Whittaker	Gynn Inn	Exors of Mrs Shuttleworth
James Gardner	Farmers Arms, Lytham Rd	Ellen Benson
John Kirby	Star Inn, Star Hills	Exors of Geo Ormerod
Saul Rowlands	Bowling Green, Bath St	Mary Hodgson
James Tattersall	Bird-in-Hand, Bolton St	Henry Gardner
Robert Wilkinson	Rising Sun, Bolton St	Robert Wilkinson
David Phillips	Bull Inn, Waterloo Rd	Richard Salthouse
Alfred Pollard	Waterloo Tavern, Cow Gap Lane	Exors of T. Shaw
Thomas Addy	Life Boat Inn	Thomas Jolly
Josias Dagger	Atlantic Inn, Fox Hall Rd	Robert Bickerstaffe
Geo. Barrett	Washington House, Fox Hall Rd	Betsey Dutton
John Wylie	South Pier Hotel	John Bickerstaffe
Joseph Buckley	Farmer's Arms, Chapel St	N.D. Worthington
John Rossall	Our House, Oddfellow St	Thomas Butler
Thomas Aspen	Concert Inn, Bonny St	Grace Wilkinson
Edward Harrison	Brunswick Hotel	Cedric Houghton
Mary Ann Phillips	Prince of Wales Arcade, Bank Hey Street	Central Property Co
Thomas Ward	White Swan Bank Hey St	John Leigh
Thomas Hacking	Welcome Inn, Bank Hey St	Cuthbert Fare
Wm Henry Jenking	Victoria Vaults, Victoria St	John E.B. Cocker
Albert Whiteside	Grapes Inn, Lytham St	John Read
Thomas Holden	New Road Inn, New Road	Occupier
Lord Heyworth	Wheat Sheaf, Lark Hill	Occupier
John Dewhurst	Golden Lion, New Road	Occupier
Edward Hoyle	Brewer's Arms, Warbreck Rd	George Slater
James Sanderson	Welcome Inn, Moss Side	Betty Whiteside
James Boardman	Lane Ends Hotel, Hawes Side	M. Brown & Co
John Thos. Bennett	Boar's Head, Gt Marton Village	Exors of John Lightbound
Thomas Lingard	Revoe Inn, Revoe	Thomas Ball

In addition to those listed, others are shown as *Letters* which apparently indicated that a licence had been granted provisionally. These are listed with the name of the applicant, but do not show a *house sign*, though the street is shown. They include 22 Bolton Street, two in Topping Street, one in West Street, three in Talbot Road and one in Talbot Square.

There were 25 *Wine & Beer* Off Licences.

BLACKPOOL DRUNKENNESS, 1886

Extracted from the Police Superintendent's Report to the Annual Licensing Meeting

	1881 Population	Estimated 1886 Population	No Licensed Victs	ON Beerhouses	OFF Beerhouses	Lic. Victs Convicted	ON Beersellers Convicted	Males Convicted	Females Convicted	Total Convicted	Total Convictions last year
Bispham with Norbreck	714	1022	3	3				1		1	2
Layton with Warbreck (Blackpool Central & South)	12711	16536	50	36	26			164	26	190	197
Marton	2303	2458	7	4				5		5	5

On 21st September 1885, Tom Lockwood, licensee of the Foxhall Hotel was prosecuted for allowing his house to open during prohibited hours. It appears that the summons was dismissed. He took possession of the licence in April 1885.

THE COST AND THE STATE OF CRIME IN BLACKPOOL, 1887-90

Each year, the Chief Constable of Blackpool or Head Constable as he was called initially, had to provide statistics to the Home Office on certain expenses and on the number of prosecutions in the past year. In the first 4 years of the Borough Force's life, when the population according to the 1881 census was 14,229, but was probably nearer 20,000, as this was a period of terrific growth in the town, the figures included:-

	Establishment	Salaries	Horses	Buildings	Total costs
1887 (3 mths only)	1 Head, 3 Sgts 16 PC's	£390.17s.9d	£8.7s.6d	£72.7s.3d	£876.6s.7d
1888	1 Head, 1 Insp 3 Sgts, 18 PC's	£1584.17s.3d	£5.0s.0d	£419.1s.1d	£2372.6s.6d
1889	-do-	£1772.12s.5d	£8.10s.0d	£405.2s.0d	£2705.11s.3d
1890	1 Head 1 Insp 3 Sgts, 25 PC's	£1854.1s.9d	NIL	£518.14s.4d	£2751.17s.8d

In the same years, the prosecution figures, at both the Police Court and at the Quarter Sessions, included the following figures:- (M = Males, F = Females)

	Known Thieves	Prostitutes	Vagrants	Habitual Drunkards	Total
1887	13M, 6F	3F	13M, 0F	2M, 0F	272M, 58 F
1888	34M, 4F	15F	27M, 5F	43M, 8F	635M, 136F
1889	36M, 9F	9F	14M, 1F	54M, 6F	752M, 155F
1890	26M, 3F	16F	27M, 7F	104M, 16F	787M, 154F

The document from which these figures were taken is to be found in the County Record Office.

STREET ACCIDENTS CAUSED BY VEHICLES IN BLACKPOOL 1911-1916

Statistics have recently come to light of the return made by the Chief Constable of Blackpool to the Home Office showing the number and type of accidents involving (the words used are *caused by*) vehicles in the years 1911/1912/1913/1914/1916. They make interesting reading when compared with today's figures, and help us recall a time when it was safe (almost) to cross the road.

The returns refer to *horse-drawn* and *mechanically-propelled* vehicles. Both sets of figures are divided into sections for omnibuses, tramcars and *other vehicles*, and into *Fatal* and *Non-fatal* (F and NF)

	Horse Drawn (All are *Other Vehicles*)	Mechanically Propelled				Total
		Omnibuses	Tramcars	Other Vehicles	Pedal Cycles	
1911	1 F 15 NF		16 NF	19 NF		51
1912	1 F 13 NF		2 F 12 NF	3 F 20 NF		51
1913	1 F 16 NF	2 NF	13 NF	1 F 21 NF		54
1914	1 F 11 NF	1 NF	15 NF	4 F 44 NF		76
1916	6 NF		3 F 16 NF	3 F 33 NF	1 F 5 NF	67

Who's for Blackpool?

Neaw then, theer; who's for Blackpool?
  Who's for a holiday?
Pack up yo'r traps, an' come, yo' chaps,
  Let's all go down to th' say.
For th' sun is shinin' breetly theer;
  No sign of fog or smook;
At Blackpool th' sky is blue an' clear.
  Who's off? Let's tak' our hook!

Yo've worked in th' mill an' th' foundry,
  An' down in th' deep, dark mine;
Fro' morn to neet, fro' dark to leet,
  Aw weathers, weet or fine.
Yo've earned a bit o' play, I think,
  So come to Blackpool's shore,
An' here enjoy yo'r meyt an' drink;
  It'll mak' yo' want lots more.

For Blackpool's breeze is famous
  For mendin' th' appetite;
It breetens th' mind of aw mankind,
  An' soon sets aw things right.
When yo're on th' Prom yo'r trouble's gone,
  It's melted by th' salt spray:
An' aw life's ills by Neptune's pills
  Are swept fair clean away.

Down theer, on th' Pier, at leisure
  Yo' may smook pipe or cigar;
An' th' wife, too, gets her pleasure—
  Yo've both forgotten th' war.
An' down on th' sands are th' childer's bands,
  Aw castle buildin' theer,
While yo' are "buildin' castles", too,
  An' Paradise seems near.

87

At th' famous "Tower" an' th' "Gardens"
Yo con both enjoy a donce,
Theer in th' Grand Pavilions,
Rememberin' yo're young once.
At th' Pleasure Beach yo' ne'er need seech
For jolly gradely fun,
For theer its found aw o'er the ground
Fro' morn till set o' sun.

An' then at neet there's th' age-old treat—
Th' sun sinkin' into th' west;
An' clouds o' glory, red an' gowd,
Are gildin' Nature's breast;
An' th' grand owd ocean sings a tune,
A soothin', gentle lay,
'At mak's a mon feel fain he's on
A blessed holiday.

This poem was written by Arthur Laycock from the *Come to Blackpool* poem by his father Sam. It appeared in altered form in the *Manchester Evening News* in 1912. This above is from Laycock's Christmas Sketches of 1920.

BLACKPOOL'S LITERARY ASSOCIATIONS
Bob Dobson

To be quite frank, Blackpool's literary associations are scant, and one needs to broaden the usual definition of that term to make anything of an essay on the subject. To this end, I propose to refer to:- a) Writers associated with Blackpool, b) those who have written about the place, especially on historical matters, and c) books which have used Blackpool as a setting.

The only Lancashire dialect writer of any note to have been born in Blackpool was *William Baron ("Bill o' Jacks") 1865-1927*, who achieved acclaim in Rochdale. He lived here for only five years, but retained a love for it. Read his poem *"A peep at mi birthplace"* in his book *"Echoes from the loom"*.

One of the "Holy Trinity" of Lancashire dialect writers, *Samuel Laycock* lived in Foxhall Road and on the Promendade near the New Inn, at the northern end of the Golden Mile from 1869 to his death in 1893. He came here for the good of his health and set up as a photographer. He was a force in the town's literary and artistic life for many years, and was made a member of the town's first Free Library committee. I specially like Sam's *"Rowl Away Theaw Grand Owd Ocean"*, surely written on the Promenade. In 1901, a group of Lancashire people formed a committee to erect a memorial statue to Sam. It seems that insufficient was raised, but in 1910, his portrait in oils was presented to the public library.

Perhaps the man who did most in his books to advertise Blackpool was *(Charles) Allen Clarke, known as "Teddy Ashton"*. He came from Bolton to Blackpool in 1901, and coined the phrase *"Windmill Land"* for the Fylde. That is the title of one of his many books. He wrote a history of the town's lifeboats, wrote a song *"Blackpool Girl"* in 1906, was prominent as a Socialist, spiritualist, writer in both dialect and standard English, publisher, journalist and cyclist. He was the most prolific writer in dialect that Lancashire has ever had. A phenomenal man, he founded the Lancashire Authors Association. When he died in 1935, it was decided to honour him and in 1936 Marton Windmill was renovated and dedicated as a permanent memorial to him. Allen Clarke was a giant of Lancashire literature.

That giant of English literature, *Charles Dickens* stayed overnight at the Imperial Hotel in 1869. He wrote of *"picking up amazingly in appetite"* though he had had to cancel a reading through ill health.

Roy Fuller (b 1912) came to Blackpool as a boy and worked here as a solicitor. Reading his book *"Souvenirs" (1980)* his love of his days here, of the Metropole Hotel, and of his Blackpool bride, come through. Forsaking his profession, he was awarded the Queen's Medal for Poetry in 1970, and for 7 years was a governor of the B.B.C. He has several books of poems, 8 novels and 2 books of memoirs to his name.

Sir Harold Riley Grime (1896-1984) is predominantly known as a journalist. Had he not chosen to be associated with the *"Evening Gazette"* he would certainly have achieved wider fame on some national newspaper. In 1950, *H.R.G.* became a Freeman of Blackpool. In that year he published *"Sand in my shoes"*, a collection of essays, mostly of his wartime thoughts. I'm sure you'll enjoy this morsel from it, and agree with me as to the quality of his writing:-

"If you come North by that train, you change at Preston, and across the Fylde you sit in darkness. Pick the right time and weather, and you will have a vista of

moon-drenched countryside to clear away the cobwebs
of the London train.
The roads are ribbons of silver, curling into the shadows
of thicket and copse. The old windmills, bereft of
arms, watch mutely over country which has altered
little with the centuries.
To the "Sand Grown 'Un", whether returning from
far-off battlefields or only from London, the thought
arises—This is worth fighting for."

Son of the revered Sam, *Arthur Laycock* was an early
Socialist councillor. He wrote several Lancashire-set
novels, including *"Warren of Manchester"* which is set in
Blackpool and Manchester of the later years of last
century. He wrote many Blackpool pieces.

"Langford Saunders" (*Peter L.B. Saunders*), lived at
Bispham for some years, and whilst there he published
"Lancashire Humour and Pathos". He was a founder
member, with *Allen Clarke,* of the Lancashire Authors
Association. He also wrote as *"Anock Butty"*. Incidentally, the book mentioned was type-set by Saunders
when he was 72 years old. It was, until recently, a
unique feat in Lancashire book production. In the prelude
to *"Mister MacFoodlum and Son, a seaside romance in*
rhyme" (1919), Saunders sets the scene:-

My scenery's laid on the north-western coast,
A seaside resort, which is Lancashire's boast;
Where motley crowds throng from myriad places
To imbibe the pure air, and bronze their wan faces.
Where the wide firmanent of ambrosial blue,
Dotted with cirrus is enchanting to view;
And the sun's rays diffuse, in grand jubilee,
Their swift-changing hues on an unruffled sea.

There varied amusement the wearied one calls
To its palaces, theatres, gardens and halls;
Where freedom from worry the spirit inspires,
And man-evolved pleasures sooth Reason's desires.
There the sea's music sings in constant refrain
Its call to the toil-worn again and again;
Where salt breezes blow, and the bosom expands
With comforting health on the fine golden sands.

The rhyme was written after Saunders and a friend were
walking on the Promenade when they saw two couples
walking past them. The two males were father and son,
and they had married two sisters.

Rochdale writer *Edwin Waugh*, renowned for his dialect

verse and stories, but master of the descriptive essay came to Blackpool, probably to see *Sam Laycock.* I recommend you to read the chapter on Norbreck in his book *"Lancashire Sketches, Pt. 2."*

Famous novelist *Edgar Wallace* fought in the 1931 election here. He didn't win, and sadly he didn't write anything against a Blackpol backdrop.

Pre-eminent as a historical writer and speaker, *Kathleen Eyre* came to St Annes from Yorkshire as a young lass, and grew to love the Fylde. Her books, particularly *"Seven Golden Miles" (1961)* are essential reading for anyone interested in old Blackpool.

Percy P. Hall, J.P. contributed *"100 years of Blackpool Education" (1970)* to our historical record. A schoolmaster, student of local history, magistrate, councillor, *"P.P."* has contributed far more to Blackpool than he could ever record.

William Hutton wrote the first history book on Blackpool, *"A description of Blackpool in Lancashire, frequented for sea-bathing"* in 1789. It was reprinted in 1800, 1804, 1817 and 1944. He was a Birmingham businessman who had brought his wife and family to this watering place in 1788 for a stay, and was so taken up by the *"good company, much pride, much vulgarity accompanied with good nature"* that he came again and became its first historian, Sadly, through *"friends"* letting him down over finances, and through printers pirating his work, he made next to nowt by his efforts.

John Porter, son of a Preston printer who had set up in Fleetwood in the early 1840's, wrote his magnificent *"History of the Fylde of Lancashire"* in 1876. He was tragically drowned in Belgium. His father's *"Fleetwood Chronicle"* was the Fylde's first newspaper.

Though not setting out as a historian or writer, through keeping a diary, *Thomas Tyldesley of Foxhall* was in fact the first true Blackpool historian. His diary, covering 1712-14 was edited and published in 1873 by Anthony Hewitson of Preston.

Reverend William Thornber was the vicar of St John's Church 1829-46 and lies there yet. He had a job "on the side" as Blackpool correspondent for the *Preston Pilot* newspaper. A native of Poulton, he wrote on the geology, history and archaeology of Blackpool and the Fylde, including *"Pennystone, a tale of the Spanish Armada"*, and of course *"Historical and Descriptive Account of Blackpool and Neighbourhood" (1837)*. He perpetuated the myth of Singleton Thorpe, and perhaps he even started it.

Thornber was certainly a character. He was not a great believer in abstinence from strong drink. Allen Clarke said of him *"Though he had his failings, he strove to do that which was righteous."*

W. Hartley Bracewell wrote *"A History of Blackpool Football Club"* in 1931, and *"A Short History of North Shore Unitarian Church"* in 1945. He was the prive mover in a fund set up to honour Samuel Laycock. His *"Tales of the Cliffs" (1904)* consists of a number of short stories, related by a Dr Cyril Winborne, most of them set in *"St Eve"* (St Annes?), which is close to *"Fairdale", "Wyrewater", "Shelborne"* and *"Millington"*. He mentions a house called *"Anchorsholme"*, and one story refers to Blackpool, the wreck of *The Foudroyant* and *"the telephone office in Abingdon Street"*.

Though the town is never named in them, certainly the novels of *"Julian Prescott"* are set right here, in the police courts, solictors' offices and drinking establishments of the town centre, for the author is really John Budd, solicitor of the highest reputation, Her Majesty's Coroner, lover of horse racing and gentleman, who has observed the Blackpool scene since his childhood in the second decade of this century.

The dialect writer *Ben Brierley* visited the town in the last half of last century. One of his stories, *"A Rainy Day at Blackpool"* tells of the jape of such a day, and another tells of *"Ab's Bathing Adventure at Blackpool"*. He probably came to see his mate Samuel Laycock.

Despite the author's remarks to the contrary in his introduction, *"Carnival at Blackport" (1937)* by *James Lonsdale Hodson* is clearly set in this resort in the first quarter of this century. I ask you—How many seaside resorts have a Tower, and *"can absorb on August Bank Holiday a quarter of a million people who don't belong here ....notwithstanding she allows them to sleep 3 in a bed and to turn her bath and billiards table into couches"*.Not many.

Dialect writers from many counties visited Blackpool and set their sketches here, including Yorkshire's *John Hartley (1839-1915)*. Read his *"Seets i' Blackpool, Fleetwood, Lytham & Southport, as seen by Sammywell Grimes an' his wife Molly on their holiday trip, wi' a few incidents an' accidents at occurrred."*

Lancashire writer *Frank Tilsley* set his novel *"Pleasure Beach* (1944) in *"Northpool, that heaven of sea and sand, of cheerful, warm vulgarity, of Movies and Dirt Trade, jazz bands and dog races, Vaudeville and clicketting turnstiles, song books and pennies-in-the-slot machines."* Highly commended.

Elizabeth Troop was born in Blackpool in 1931 and now lives in London. Her novel *"Darling Daughters" (1981 Granada)* is set in the town before, during and after the Second World War. There have been many novels whose action takes place here, but I fear I can't list them all.

Although the *"Selsby"* of *Paul Williams'* book *"The Knights of Selsby" (1934)* is built on the estuary of a river, it clearly is Blackpool. The book went into four editions before 1938, and concerns two gentlemen of the town who eventually become *"Sirs"*. The writer obviously had some legal connections here.

I can't ascertain how *Jerome K. Jerome (1859-1927)* came to know Blackpool, but he said of it, *"Blackpool is a watering-place among a thousand for harmless fun, frivolity and gaiety"*. We do know that his plays were produced here during his lifetime. His play, *"The Passing of the Third Floor Back"* had been a flop when introduced to Harrogate audiences, but his agent wired him on the first night of it opening here *"It's all right. Blackpool loves and understands it."*

I hope I've given you a taste for reading how various writers have viewed and interpreted Blackpool through their pens and typewriters.

SOME SUGGESTED READING: In no special order

Eyre, Kathleen	Seven Golden Miles (1961 & 1975) Byegone Blackpool (1971)
Prescott, Julian	Both Sides of the Case (1958); Case Proceeding (1960); Case for Trial (1962)
Walton, J.K.	The Blackpool Landlady (1978)
Parry, Keith	Resorts of the Lancashire Coast (1983)
Clegg, John Trafford	Sketches & Rhymes in the Rochdale Dialect, Vol 1 (1895)
Palmer & Turner	Victorian Blackpool (1975); Blackpool by Tram (1968, 1978); The Blackpool Pleasure Beach Story (1978); Blackpool's Heyday (1979); By Tram to the Tower (1965); Edwardian Blackpool, a tour by tram (1974); Picture Postcards from Blackpool & the Fylde Coast 1898-1939 (1980); Trams & Buses around Blackpool
Moore, Henry	Bibliography of works of Charles Allen Clarke (1972)
Gribble, L.	They kidnapped Stanley Matthews (197?) Novel
Curry, Avon	Hunt for Danger (1974 Milton House) Novel
Enefer, Douglas	Girl In A Million (1970 Hale) Novel
Francis, Richard	Blackpool Vanishes (1979 Faber & Faber) Science Fiction

Hardcastle, Michael	Goals In The Air (1972 Heinemann) Soccer novel
Yates, E.M.	Blackpool, A.D. 1533. Essay in Geographical Journal 1961
Sholto, Anne	Evening Primrose (1952); Gate by the Shore (1954); House with the blue door (1952) Romances
Ellis, Ron	Murder First Class (1980 Hale) Novel
Whittle, Peter	Marina, an historical & descriptive account of Southport, Lytham & Blackpool (1831)
Fishwick, Col. Henry	History of Bispham Parish (1887 Chetham Society) He also wrote on the parishes of Lytham, Kirkham, Poulton
Hirst, George	The Golden Mile (1974 Sphere) Novel
Kneeshaw, John W.	A Black Shadow (189?) Lancashire tale
Kendrick, T.D.	Great Love for Icarus (1962 Methuen) Novel
Murray, D.L.	Leading Lady (1947) Theatrical novel
Perrett, Jennie	Ben Owen, a Lancashire Story (c1890)
Verrells, Sgt. H.V.	Spud Wilkins at Blackpool (1918 Blackpool) Fiction
Pastil, Peter	Rural Studies in the Westmorland Dialect (1868 Kendal); In this is a story set in *The Brighton of the North*
Longworth, D.	The Visit of Mr & Mrs Jeremiah Grubb and family to Blackpool....(1865 Preston)
Brierley, Ben	Drop't on at Blackpool (c1880) Dialect
Grime (Editor)	A Scientific Survey of Blackpool & District, prepared for the British Association, 1936
Clarke, A. Allen	Windmill Land (1916, 1933, 1986); More Windmill Land (1918); Windmill Land Stories (1924); The Story of Blackpool Lifeboat (1924); The Story of Blackpool (1923); Tales of old Blackpool & the Fylde (1908); History of Blackpool (1926)
Stott, Alan	Layton Village (1980); History of Norbreck & Little Bispham (1982)
Green, John	Marton through the centuries (1976); Ten Generations
Desborough, Harry H.F	The Hunchback of Blackpool ( ) Novel
Roeder, Charles	Blackpool: a sketch of its rise & growth 1592-1792 (1903 Antiquarian Soc of Lancs & Cheshire)
Dobson, Scott	The Blackpool Book (Frank Graham 1971)
Smith, W. John	Blackpool: a sketch of its growth 1740-1851 (1959 Historic Society of Lancashire & Cheshire)
Britton	Beauties of England & Wales (1807) - The Lancashire chapter
Hyde, J.	Blackpool of Today. Essay in The Windsor Magazine, July-December 1896
Whittle, P.	An historical and descriptive account of Blackpool (1851)

Last, a tip—The index files in the Blackpool Central Library Reference Room are a mine of information.

THE PLEASURE BEACH   by Doreen Brotherton

Eight million visitors a year testify to the popularity of
one of Blackpool's greatest attractions—the Pleasure
Beach. Covering an area of more than forty acres, its
claim to be Europe's foremost funfair is not disputed, and
its appeal seems to be almost universal.

The south end of Blackpool, to which thousands now
flock in search of thrills, was still a barren waste when
the central and north shore areas had latched on to the
holiday bandwaggon. When in 1894 the promenade was
extended to reach the Victoria (now South) Pier, there
was little in the way of entertainment for those who
ventured *to the end of the line*. A troupe of nigger
minstrels entertained with song and dance on fine days
and there was a skittle alley and hobby horses. You could
also have your *bumps* read by the phrenologist Ellis
family who advised on health, work and affairs of the
heart: get a daguerreotype holiday memento at the photo-
graphic booth, or enjoy an icecream at Mr Pye's stall.

Before 1910 the area was essentially the domain of the
gypsies, encamped in blanket tents or the occasional
vardo, living off the land or earning what they could
from their strange powers of clairvoyance and sixth sense.
Fortunately one of their number, Sylvester Gordon
Boswell, has written his autobiography, *The Book of
Boswell* (published by Victor Gollancz 1970). Boswell was
born in 1895. His father was, in the season, the manager of
a primitive "figure of eight" and scenic railway, his
brother earned a meagre living repairing the cars and
track, whilst female relatives read the palms of those willing to part with their silver. Recalling memories of the
embryo pleasure beach of 1899, Boswell writes,

*Now another amusement on the beach at that time, as I
remember, was one old set of Gallopers (roundabout) and
they belonged to old Charlie Outhwaite. And there used
to be a figure-board and if you rode on the outside—on the
third row of horses—and you reached out, there was some
rings on this figure-board, and if you could put your finger
in a ring and show it to the man who took the money, you
could get an extra ride. And there was another sort of
Galloper-track—but with bicycles on it three abreast—and
people used to get on this and pedal themselves along, and
the more people that was on, the faster they went. And that
was a penny a ride. That was about the only amusements
there was on South Shore, Blackpool, apart from gypsy
women with the palmistry business. And I don't remember*

anything else apart from the old bathing machines that used to be pulled with a horse, backwards and forwards.

At that time most of the infant pleasure beach was owned by William George Bean who had brought the *Hotchkiss Bicycle* from America. He and John Outhwaite went into partnership in the early years of this century. It was Bean's avowed aim to create an amusement park which would *"make adults feel like children again."*

When the Pleasure Beach Company was formed in 1910, a bye-law was passed to evict the gypsies from the South Shore site. It also declared, *no person following the calling of clairvoyant, phrenologist, palmist or quack doctor or any person pretending or professing to tell fortunes or use any subtle craft, means or device by palmistry or otherwise, to deceive or impose on any of His Majesty's subjects shall be permitted on any part of the land set aside as a Fair Ground.*

Presumably it was no concern of Blackpool Corporation if deception were perpetrated on foreigners!

William George Bean devoted the rest of his life to his dream of a magnificent pleasure park on the style of those already popular in America. By the time he died in 1929 he had, with the help of an American *ride* expert, transformed the sandy wasteland of the nineteenth century. *The Pleasure Beach Amusement Park* had become one of Blackpool's main attractions. Already there was the *wedding cake* casino near the entrance, described by Allen Clarke as *a White Palace by the sea.* The Casino itself embraced a restaurant, a billiard hall and cinema and beyond it were diversions such as Noah's Ark, River Caves, Scenic Railway, a flying machine, Big Dipper, water shute, helter skelter, coconut shies, ice-cream stalls—even a free *motor park* for the wealthy. At night strings of fairy lights illuminated the whole complex—a fairground unique in this country.

After the death of Bean, his son-in-law Leonard Thompson took control of the developing fairground and literally changed its image with the assistance of the architect Joseph Emberton who redesigned much of the site to give the modern pleasure beach its distinctive look. One of his finest achievements was the completely new style Casino at the entrance, and it was Emberton who designed the original Fun House and the Grand National.

Perhaps not all the later buildings emulate Emberton's architecturally brilliant fusion of form and function, but the success story of Blackpool's Pleasure Beach has continued to escalate. New rides and attractions are added every year. Amongst current favourites are the ever popular Log Flume, and the Tidal Wave, said to simulate the experience of sailors in the South Pacific where, after tropical storms, a crew's endurance was tested as the boat was carried high on gigantic waves and then almost to the bottom of the sea. It's a surprisingly popular recipe for sea-sickness! Other recent additions are the Revolution, where intrepid holiday-makers enjoy the thrill of whirling at speed through 360 degrees, and the Tokaydo Express which travels in a figure 8 on an undulating track at breathtaking velocity.

There are now more than 150 rides to suit all ages. There's something new every year. The atmosphere of the Pleasure Beach assails—even assaults—the senses. There's more to it than the raucous noise of screaming enjoyment, the grinding and clattering of machinery, the smell of hamburgers, chips and doughnuts, the flashing lights or the infectious laughter of those in search of *white knuckle* thrills and excitement. The carnival atmosphere here lasts all through the season. It's unusual to see a miserable face at the Pleasure Beach, and if a funfair can claim that, with eight million visitors a year, there must be something very special about it.

THE BLACKPOOL ILLUMINATIONS

by Harry Carpenter, Director of Street Lighting and
Electrical Services, 1949-73

Blackpool was the first town in Britain to have electric street lighting along its promenade. It was introduced as a late-season attraction rather than for public safety in late August 1879. Eight arc-lamps—six on the promenade and one on each of the then two piers—provided a floodlit arena for the opening Carnival Night, which attracted a crowd of 100,000 visitors from all over the country. Considering the transport problems of those days, it was a remarkable success story. The initial cost of those lights was £3,500, but the money was recovered during the opening fete alone. I quote from a Gas Lighting Journal of September, 1879:-

Electricity may be the champagne light on fete days, but coal gas is the Bass' beer light of everyday life; and though the former is not to be despised on occasions, the latter is wholesomer, not to mention cheaper of the two, and what most sensible people prefer to use.....(its success) only serves to prove its utter impracticability as a general illuminant and the impossibility of its ever, in the slightest degree, competing with, or interfering with the progress of gas lighting......

What can be identified as the first Blackpool Illuminations really began with the Civic decorations for the visit of H.M. Princess Louise to open a new section of the promenade in May 1912. Strings of fairy lights through the gardens, up the flagpoles and across triumphal arches marked a significant break through from the previous pattern of lighted buildings and tramcars. So successful was this spectacle that it was re-staged in September and October of that year as an Autumn attraction. Blackpool lights were born, and a more ambitious scheme (of 60,000 lamps) made the 1913 season the most successful Blackpool had ever known. The 1914 display held even greater promise, but the outbreak of war drastically curbed Blackpool's season, and the illuminations were not to be seen again for another ten years.

Electricity supplies were limited after the war, so Blackpool tried a Carnival Week—on the lines of the famous Nice spectacle—as an early season attraction for 1923 and 1924. In 1925, the Council decided to spend £2,600 on a new illuminations display, and Blackpool's *Autumn Lights* sparked again. Freddie Field, an Assistant Electrical Engineer under Cornelius Quinn and later under Charles

Furness, was the guiding influence, and to him goes the main credit for pioneering and developing successive displays, on an increasing scale, until the outbreak of War in 1939. Equipment was dismantled and stored for another ten years.

In 1949, fuel restrictions were relaxed, and the pre-war equipment trooped out of retirement, looking fresh and original to a new generation. That year's display was again handled by Freddie Field.

I came on the scene in late 1949 to stage the 1950 display at a cost of £75,000—a shattering figure then to many people. What a headache I inherited: old, worn-out equipment, archaic workshops and no real organisation existing. So I set out to lay a firm foundation for future lights, based on a team of selected employees working to a set programme throughout the year. The opposite of the larger, seasonal work-force which had been used previously. A new electricity distribution system was planned, with adequate transformer sub-stations and supply points. Easier and safer erection arrangements were formulated, with mechanical handling devices, and site provision made so that equipment would withstand those Autumn gales.

New display techniques had to be introduced—more suited to post-war tastes. New equipment and tableaux were devised, using modern materials and manufacturing techniques. The display was developed and extended as circumstances permitted. One breakthrough was the introduction of glass-fibre for making the display features. Its use for this purpose was pioneered at Blackpool. Always, over the years, there was that nagging challenge that, each successive year the display had to be better than the last—despite the budget. With the aid of an enthusiastic design team, which of course changed from time to time, I was able to successfully stage a series of displays for those twenty-four years (1950 to 1973) which helped to maintain and embellish the Blackpool Story.

One tends to forget the many human, physical and financial problems which are a daily ingredient of every management post. Even the inevitable annual battle in the municipal committees and council to justify an ever-increasing budget. One conveniently overlooks mistakes, such as when I erected some *Juggling Clowns* over the Town Hall, which soon became known as *the Clown Hall*. Needless to say, when it was said that this depicted the Mayor and Chairman of the Finance Committee juggling with the town's finances, I was told to take it down. One tries to forget that particular opening night when the first 700-yards long tableau I had created was blown down and wrecked in a gale; and the year when I introduced a sprayed plastic as a display medium for twelve large, internally-illuminated parrots, and these were ripped open in a gale. (The plastic was the same as that used to cocoon the fleet after the war). I try to forget too the time when I first introduced fireworks for the Switch-on-Ceremony, and everyone thought the fuses had blown. Maybe it was the Switch-on when we had an electricians' strike for several weeks, and although I had made certain tentative arrangements for the night, I only received a note saying they would return to work just as the TV cameras focussed on me for the opening of an interview in Talbot Square.

I think of the personalities I have had the pleasure of meeting on radio and TV interviews—Richard Dimbleby, Wynford Vaughan Thomas and Barney Colehan. I recall too the interlude with Harry Secombe on a particularly windy night on the North Shore cliffs, and I shall never forget *Professor* Stanley Unwin instructing me in *the trickly-how of amp an'volten.*

Once, the Daily Mail carried a double-column headline announcing that I *did my best work in bed.* The story of how displays emerged had not been sufficiently news-worthy until I mentioned the notepad I kept alongside my bed to record my ideas on awaking. It took quite a time to live that one down.

There are those nostalgic memories of Switch-on Nights and the long list of personalities who have featured at those ceremonies. Memories too of the detailed planning for a day always spent with fingers crossed and butter-flies in the tummy. We had to arrange an organ for Reg Dixon, arrange for a shy Stanley Matthews to be smuggled out of the back door of the Town Hall, and had problems with the irascible Gilbert Harding. Violet Carson was lovely even with her Ena Sharples hair-net, and so was Gracie Fields in her shawl. Her husband Boris was an electrician and was anxious to see the works. The night that Jayne Mansfield switched on, a man ran for 5 miles alongside the Civic tram to keep her in view. For the Russian ambassador, Jacob Malik, we bought a bottle of vodka, only to learn he drank whisky.

My "finest hour" was the Switch-on from an R.A.F. Canberra flying over the Promenade at 310 m.p.h. This took precise and detailed planning over several months with the R.A.F., the Battle of Britain aces and the film artistes. On the day, we had a specially-equipped control station operating from the attic of the Town Hall, and two Canberras (one on standby over Barrow).

The use of light for ceremonies and festivities is as old as the hills. The Chinese are first credited with using ornamental lanterns for social events, and the mystical qualities of light and fire have been used throughout the ages. Light is fascinating, and possesses strong powers of attraction (as moths know). Natural and artificial light exerts a powerful influence on all our activities (as humans know). It affects our moods, our emotions and it tempers our thoughts and outlook. For success, one must always design for the interest and appreciation of the public at large, whilst to satisfy the Civic Fathers, the motto has always been "Marry a little money with a lot of ingenuity". The latter costs nothing.

Today, the display extends over 6 miles of the Promenade, and makes use of equipment worth over two million pounds. It operates for about 60 nights, from late August to the end of October. There are over 150 miles of festoon strip and cables, and about 700 tons of display material. Practically all of the work is designed and produced in the 3-acre depot. The staff of around 95 employees includes designers, artists, joiners, glass-fibre workers, electricians and painters. The annual cost of producing and staging the display is around £900,000 (I remember well the time when "the budget will only go above £100,000—over my dead body"). However, expenditure is off-set in many ways; by a Businessmen's Appeal Fund, by the Collection Boxes along the Promenade, by a little commercial advertising, by the sale of surplus equipment, and through other benefits such as income accruing to the Municipal Services through tram fares, deck chair hirings and car park fees.

Blackpool Illuminations are often described as "The Greatest Free Show on Earth". Besides its ever-increasing popularity and vital importance to Blackpool, it is also a viable business proposition for the Local Authority. To spend some nine-tenths of a million pounds gross (but only about one-quarter nett) to maintain an established Autumn attraction which attracts business estimated at over £60 million is surely worthwhile. And this when other resorts have put up their shutters for the Winter.

I believe that, with new media, advancing techniques, experience and expertise, this form of lighting will continue to "glow" for many years ahead.

Extract from Official Blackpool Guide, 1906

BRILLIANT LIGHTING

The effect produced after dusk, when the full brilliance of the Municipal and private installations is being displayed, is such as to carry the mind to occasions of the highest festival. In the use of electricity Blackpool acted as the pioneer of British seaside resorts. It graced the now demolished promenade with powerful arc lamps as far back as 1879—when electricity as an illuminant was in its infancy—and, in 1893, in honour of electricity being extended throughout the Borough for public street lighting and for private use, a more liberal and elaborate scheme of Promenade illumination was inaugurated by that eminent electrical scientist, Lord Kelvin. The magnificent effect then brought about has been intensified and extended in connection with the entirely new promenade. Artistic columns, bearing the latest arc lamps, are fixed, at short intervals, from end to end of the vast sea parades, and, as the brilliancy of this famous line of light is added to by the illuminations of the Piers and the huge places of entertainment the charms of the Blackpool front after nightfall quite correspond with the delights of the day. The whole of the principal throughfares—from North Shore to South Shore—are also brightly lighted with electric arcs, and, as almost the whole of the window-featured tradesmen's establishments further contribute to the town's brightness, the setting of the sun merely serves as the signal for an artificial radiance such as is rarely met with in the most advanced Municipalities.

Quote from a Lancashire dialect writer of a hundred years ago

He wor aggreably supproiset, on turnin' out t'fost neet, to see t'promanade an' booath pier yeds li up by nine electrhric leets, makin' it look as leet as day.

Joe wondert however they would get to t'top o' those heigh powes to leet 'em, an' he went for three weeks hondrunnin' to see 'em leeted.

At last, he wur rewarded by seein' aw 't nine lamps lit at once, without th' aid of a lamp-leeter, but it took 'im so mich by surproise that he rush't off as hard as he could run to come an' tell us that the divvel wur in th'lectric leets an' he'd turned lampleeter. An' he wur under that impresshun till he went to t'teawn's yard one neet an' seed 'em manifracthrin t'new electricity to keep t'lamps brunnin'.

A historic picture, taken 8th July 1929, showing the first passengers to be flown to the Isle of Man from Blackpool. They left Blackpool at 5.30 p.m. and arrived at Derby Haven at 6.45 p.m., flying back at 7.30 p.m. and arriving at 8.20 p.m. Photo given by Mr Ayrton, whose father is the one with the stick.

BLACKPOOL FOOTBALL CLUB   by Gerry Wolstenholme

My affinity with Blackpool FC started when my dad used to take me into the West Stand to watch Reserve games in 1954-55. It was only Reserve games because as a young lad it was too much of a crush to go to anything more in those days! However by season 1955-56 I was big enough to go to Division 1 games and my first taste of this was an encouraging 5-1 win over Newcastle and the 'Pool ending the season as runners up to Manchester United. How times have changed, but how did it all start?

Blackpool FC were founded in July 1887. The club formed following a meeting at the Stanley Arms in Church Street on 26 July 1887 at which Fred Nickson was appointed President and Sam Bancroft Chairman of the Committee.

They played their games at the Raikes Hall Ground where following a 2-1 defeat at Chorley they beat Leek 4-1 in the first home game. The first season saw them hold their own in the League and win the Fylde Cup, beating Lytham 5-1 in front of 3000 spectators and the Lancs Junior Cup after beating Preston (A) in the semi-final.

The following season both Cups were forfeited but the game of football was very popular, there were large crowds and a net profit on the season of £60.

Blackpool were one of the founders of the Lancashire League in 1890 with South Shore FC joining the following year. Champions in 1893/94, they were not re-elected after the 1895/96 season. Interest had waned, results were bad but on 13 May 1896 Alderman John Bickerstaffe decided something had to be done. He presided over a meeting at which Blackpool Football Company was formed with capital of 2000 £1 shares, and Blackpool were elected to the 2nd Division of the Football League. Here therefore starts Blackpool FC as it is today with all the trials and tribulations, hopes, ambitions, fears and disappointments, struggles for promotion and against relegation to come. The first season ended with the team 8th in the League, having won their first cup tie, they were knocked out in the following round by Newton Heath (Man Utd) after an away draw. Financially the season was not a success as there was a loss of £1182.

Mediocrity followed with 11th position in 1897/98 and 16th position the following season. Unfortunately the bottom 3 teams had to seek re-election and they were Blackpool (20 pts), Loughborough (19 pts) and Darwen (9 pts). Loughborough remained but Middlesborough and Chesterfield replaced Blackpool and Darwen.

It was back to the Lancashire League but one momentous decision was taken; one week after beating South Shore 1-0 at Raikes Hall, the 2 teams combined, as it was felt that there was need for only one team on the Fylde Coast. Blackpool football at Bloomfield Road commenced. The team were voted back to the Football League 2nd Division after only one season away.

From then up to World War 1 they remained a middle-order team with a high of 7th place in 1910-11 and a low of 16th and re-election in 1908/09. Great players of the era were Harold Hardman, Marshall McEwan, Bob Birket, Edgar Chadwick, Jack Parkinson and Jackie Cox. The latter was the first Blackpool FC player to be selected for an international when he represented England at Outside Left.

Guests played for many league teams during WW1 but, unlike WW2, Blackpool were not well represented. However in the first season after the first war, football was booming. Blackpool cashed in with record revenue of £23000 (£17300 from gate receipts).

Mid-table obscurity followed but money was pulled in on some large transfers when George Wilson (later to captain England), Joe Lane and Peter Quinn went for a combined sum of just over £10,000.

The first of the great escapes followed in 1921/22 when despite having Harry Bedford (signed from Notts Forest in March 1921) as both team and League leading goal-scorer they had to win their last 2 games to avoid relegation. This they did beating West Ham home and away, dooming others to the drop.

The 1922/23 season saw one of the great names of football as manager, Major Frank Buckley. He stayed with the team until May 1927 and despite losing money each year (£2500-£4000) he saw them finish 4th 3 times in 5 seasons, and also reach the 4th round of the cup for the first time.

After ground improvements in 1925, Jimmy Hampson was signed from Nelson in October 1927 for around £2000. Another name in Blackpool folk lore had arrived.

In 1930 the incredible happened. On the back of 45 goals from Jimmy Hampson (he was to score 247 in 360 games for Blackpool) Blackpool were Division 2 champions and on their way to the 1st Division. A record gate of 23,868 (receipts £1825) saw them beat Oldham 3-0. Along with Hampson, Albert Watson, Percy Downes (12 goals from outside left) and Bill Tremelling were stars of the promotion winning team. Their limitations were ruth-lessly exposed once they were in the 1st Division and although they scored reasonably heavily the defence leaked 123 goals including 10 against Huddersfield.

As the last day of the season dawned they needed 1 point to stay up. Losing 2-1 to Manchester City with 10 minutes left to play all looked lost but Albert Watson blasted in a 20 yarder with just 7 minutes left to play. The 2-2 draw ensured their 1st Division life line for another season.

The following season everything once again depended on the final match and this time they won 3-1 at Sheffield United to avoid relegation yet again. The following season saw them relegated to Division 2. They spent money in an attempt to regain 1st Division status. Bert Thomson, a Scottish international outside right, Tom Jones, Bob Dougall, Sam Jones, Peter Doherty, Jock Wallace, Dick Witham and Alan Hall from Spurs were all purchased. They forsook their Tangerine strip for a season, playing in dark and light blue. However there was a loss of £15,124 on the season—the overdraft had risen to £19,515—and promotion was not gained.

In 1935 Joe Smith, a legendary figure arrived. He made changes, the most successful of which was to revert Bob Finan to centre forward from where he scored 34 goals. When promotion was missed, to make ends meet they were obliged to sell Peter Doherty to Manchester City for £10,000.

However the following season, (1936-37) all was well. 7 points clear at the top at Christmas, they needed to beat Doncaster (doomed to the 3rd) to take the title. A 1-1 draw saw Leicester City take the championship but as runners-up Blackpool were back in the First Division.

The team struggled in their first season back in Division 1 and the overdraft climbed to a pre-war high of £30,000.

In the late 1930s they acquired 3 players for no cost, Harry Johnston, Jimmy Blair and the third was a thin pale-faced boy from South Shields—Stan Mortenson who arrived for a £10 signing-on fee. As war broke out Blackpool were top of Division 1 with the only 100% record in the League; Played 3 won 3.

War-time football featured some of Blackpool's greatest moments to date. Armed with guest players, Jock Dodds (66 goals), Ronnie Dix (33 goals) and Charlie Jones (31 goals) they won the 1941/42 Northern League Championship. In the process the Burnley goalkeeper conceded 28 goals in 3 games as Blackpool beat them 9-0, 6-0 and 13-0.

In 1942-43 they lost the war time cup final to Sheffield Wednesday, and in 1943 featured in one of the all-time great games when for the Championship of England they overcame the mighty Arsenal 4-2 after being 0-2 down after 10 minutes.

Stanley Matthews (a war time guest) was signed from Stoke after the war for £11,000 and in the 1947/48 season 8 teams broke their ground attendance record when playing Blackpool; everyone wanted to see the Wizard of the Dribble.

Wembley was reached in 1948 when, in a tremendous final Manchester United triumphed 4-2. Average league seasons followed and another Wembley appearance ended in a 2-0 defeat by Newcastle United in 1951. However their finest hour was to follow when in the most-talked-about Cup Final of all, (1953) Blackpool defeated Bolton 4-3 with a Mortensen hat-trick and a last minute Perry goal. The team returned home in triumph.

In 1956-57 they achieved their highest League position for a completed season when they were runners up to Manchester United. Thereafter began an almost annual fight against relegation culminating in the drop to Division 2 in 1966-67.

Since the winning of the Cup many of Blackpool's great names appeared for the Club—Harry Johnston (retiring in 1955 after 20 years with the club), Stan Mortensen, Stan Matthews, Bill Perry, Ernie Taylor, Jackie Mudie, George Farm, Eddie Shimwell, Allan Brown, Jimmy Armfield (who completed most of his record 568 games for the club in this period), Ray Charnley and also some of the less well-sung heroes such as Roy Gratrix, David Durie, Bruce Crawford, John MacPhee, Tommy Garrett, Ray Parry and many more.

Alan Ball joined as a 17 year old in 1962 before being transferred to Everton for £112,000, a then record fee between 2 British clubs.

Emlyn Hughes also appeared briefly for the team in the sixties before being spotted by Liverpool.

After 3 years in Division 2 Blackpool regained promotion but after a season of only 4 victories they went straight back down.

This was a prelude to Blackpool's darkest hour as, after finishing in the top 10 for 6 seasons, they gradually declined so that in 1978-79 they found themselves in Division 3. They only remained there a couple of seasons before dropping to Division 4.

After finishing only mid-table in their first season they eventually had the ignominy of applying for re-election. A selection of managers and club chairmen guided them

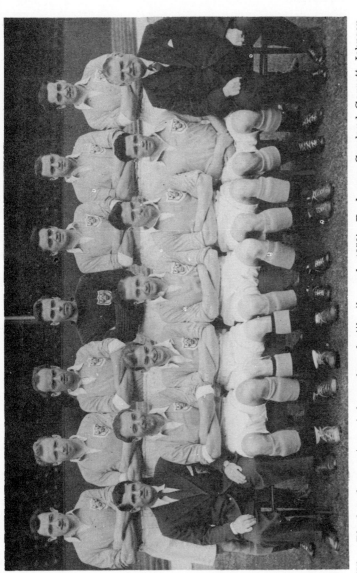

When Blackpool was a team to be reckoned with - the early 1950's. **Back row**: Crosland, Garrett, Johnson, Farm, Hayward, Shimwell, Kelly: **Front row**: Lynas (trainer), Matthews, Taylor, Mortensen, Brown, Perry, Smith (Manager)

through these unstable times but the arrival of Sam Ellis saw some stability back to the team. He has guided them back to Division 3, but who knows what the future holds as the club prepare to celebrate their hundredth birthday?

BLACKPOOL REFLECTIONS   by Allan Prior

I can't remember who they were playing but the first match I ever saw the 'Pool play they had the great Jimmy Hampson in the forward-line. Somehow, Jimmy was Blackpool in those days, a hero to schoolboys like me. A stocky man with short, wiry hair, and a terrific right-foot shot. He was daring and dashing, the spirit of Blackpool. Jimmy seemed to be in **all** those pre-war teams. And I'm not sure if he wasn't just as effective at the very end of his career, when he had Peter Doherty and Bobby Finan with him!

I saw some great goals at Blackpool (including Albert Watson's free-kick that kept Blackpool in Division One), but the one I remember best was a flying header by Bobby Finan (at the time when **nobody** performed flying headers) at the South Stand End. I don't know who that was against either, and Bobby can't remember, because I've asked him!

It would be useless to try to remember which were the good games played by the one and only Peter Doherty — they were all good, and many of them were great. For the younger fans Doherty was something like Rodney Marsh crossed with Franny Lee. He could dribble, pass **and** shoot. He was, quite simply, the best inside-forward I have ever seen.

I once remarked to Louis Cardwell (with George Farrow, one of the best uncapped players on the 'Pool's books) that Peter was a good player: and Louis said, "No, he wasn't. He was a great player."

That about sums it up.

I don't know how Tuffnell and Longden and Percy Maggs and "Shippy" and T.W. Jones would shape in fast, modern football, but they were, one and all great characters of the 'Thirties. You knew they were on the field. They walked on to Bloomfield Road as if they owned it, and they did battle in mud and gale, year in and year out. The crowds knew them by their first names, like brothers.

110

They seemed (to a schoolboy) like a Tower itself, part of the landscape, something that would never change.

But the war came, and it all **did** change. The halycon years of Blackpool Football Club lay ahead—the exciting seasons after the War, when the 'Pool had the best forward line in the league, probably in the world, for a season or so, certainly the best club line I've ever seen: Matthews, Taylor, Mortensen, Brown, Perry!

They swept down towards the Kop like a wave from the sea, and they were about as unstoppable.

But, even by then, football was beginning to change. Method football (I **hate** it!) and running about to no end and work-rate, and the domination of teams by the coaches . . . all that was on its way, equally unstoppable.

So when I think of Blackpool Football Club I think back to a stocky figure running out from the Kop End to cries of "Unload him, Shippy" and of Hampson flashing past the backs, or Doherty pushing his slow penalty kicks into the corner of the net.

And of the arguments on the Kop and of the time a friend of mine (himself not young) argued with an old fisherman as to which of them could remember furthest back, in Blackpool Football Club's history.

"Dusta remember Billy Myerscough?" my friend asked the old fisherman, casting his memory back as far as it would go.

"Billy Myerscough?" replied the salt, taking a foul pipe out of his mouth, "Ah remember his bluddy feyther!"

That was Blackpool.

GOAL SCORING. Blackpool's highest scoring draw in any first-team competition was 5-5 at Swansea in the Second Division in 1928/29.

★　★　★　★　★

NINEPENCE, A SHILLING, ONE AND SIX AND TWO SHILLINGS
Reminiscences of Blackpool Cinemas
by Jack Nelson

This is not an obituary on the Blackpool cinema but a celebration of it. It is paradoxical that that which directly led to the demise of the cinema, or, more precisely, cinema-going, has, at least, led to the preservation of the past. But for television it would no longer be possible to see the films of the 1930's, 40's and 50's as a result of the almost complete closure of the cinema house. Those cinemas that remain are to a great extent incapable of projecting films as they were intended to be seen and indeed have very few contemporary films worth screening. Sadly, the lesser of two evils remains the television receiver.

Still, at least the television receiver allows us to see and re-live the performances and productions of the great days of the cinema. The presentation and ambience of cinema-going at its best remains in the imagination but, thankfully, those fortunate enough to have experienced such are usually blessed with instant recall. I am no exception.

Perhaps the best example of presentation and ambience which can be recollected locally is the **Odeon**, Dickson Road, now operating as three cinemas but bearing little resemblance to its former glory. Originally opened in 1939 in the grand Oscar Deutsch design familiar in most large towns, the Odeon, with its beautiful lines, curvatures and floodlit tower was a prime example of modern styling. This superb cinema held over 3,500 patrons and the staff included two page boys, sixteen usherettes, nine commissionaires and six projection staff. An organ was eventually installed, the first organist being Mr Al Bollington who rose and fell as and when required amidst a blaze of technicoloured lighting. The whole design of the cinema reflected the best of the 1930's *"Astaire-Rogers"* style and I recollect that even the two auditorium clocks were without numbers. The stage itself on the opening night held the entire band of the 1st Battalion Royal Scots Guards. Two sets of curtains concealed the screen, one set directly in front of the screen and the other more grand and larger filled the whole of the proscenium. Great use was made of the curtains to create theatrical atmosphere. Effective lighting was much in evidence and each curtain would be used several times during the performance in particular to prevent the audience from being subjected to the unforgivable sin of a blank screen.

112

The opening film was *Three Smart Girls* **starring the** immensely popular Deanna Durbin by whom the audience would have been quite willingly sung to death. For all this the normal prices of admission were 9d, 1/-, 1/6d and 2/-.

However, local style and atmosphere was not confined to the mighty. Many will recollect the **Clifton Palace** on Church Street. This quaint cinema accentuated its quaintness by means of reusable metal discs for admission tickets. Further delights were revealed when it was discovered access to the circle was via a grand staircase which led up directly from the stalls. Patrons were able to ascend the entire length of the staircase over the very heads of stalls patrons and the entire length was lit by torch like lamps which would not have disgraced the Paris Opera. Some say the staircase was formerly installed in an ocean liner and whilst this has not been verified the thought gave added interest to the cinema. Patrons thrived on a diet of Charlie Chan until eventually tastes became grander and the Clifton Palace became the **Tatler News Theatre.** The transformation can best be described as Dorothy stepping from a monochrome house into the technicoloured land of Oz. Plush and comfort reigned. The staircase was walled in and now led to the circle cafe which attracted the 1950's equivalent of the 1980's jet set. But it was the seating that is best remembered. Armchair comfort was promised, and indeed provided, with sufficient room between rows for patrons to pass without disturbing those already seated. All public areas were deeply carpeted which was then a rarity in all but first-run cinemas. For me, the Tatler came into its own on Sunday nights when it was possible between 7 p.m. and 10 p.m. to languish in a Warner Bros. double bill which left patrons almost fainting with anticipation when it was discovered Sydney Greenstreet and Peter Lorre featured in both. On other than Sundays the Tatler provided continuous performances of news and interest items containing such delicacies as *Pete Smith Specialities* when fifteen hilarious minutes would be given over to whether the lady should walk on the inside or outside of the gentleman, a *Fitzpatrick Travelogue ... and so we say farewell to beautiful ... etc. etc....* —and if one was extremely fortunate a Stan Laurel and Oliver Hardy re-issue. National and international news was provided by amongst many others, *British Movietone—Lionel Gamlin reporting —Paramount,—the eyes and ears of the world— Pathe— cock-a-doodle-doo—* and the prestigious *March of Time.*

Readers are now advised to press their instant recall

buttons, as during the interval we shall have a tour of local cinemas recalling aspects which particularly remind the author of them. **The Rendezvous**, Bond Street, with its delicious smell of fresh coffee served in the foyer cafe, **the Regent,** Church Street, whose house lights were extinguished like a clap of thunder leaving unseated patrons marooned in the blackness, possibly with a cup of tea in their hands. The **King Edward**, Central Drive, whose kiosk shutter situated alongside the screen would be raised with an almighty clatter during the last two minutes of a tear jerker such as *Random Harvest* and the sorting of the dandelion and burdock commenced. The usherette at the **Palace**, Bank Hey Street, who could walk backwards the entire length of the centre aisle with a loaded tray of tea and biscuits and then return and collect the cups and saucers which patrons had kindly passed to the end of each row as requested by the slide projected during the interval. The smell of the disinfectant at the **Empire**, Hawes Side Lane and the Glen Miller records seemingly played constantly at the **Waterloo**, Waterloo Road.

It is perhaps also interesting to remember that cinemas normally showed films from particular production companies and consequently discerning film-goers quickly became patrons of a particular cinema as a result of the type of films that would be shown. For instance, the **Odeon** would have the first runs of the more prestigious offerings from Universal and Paramount, the **Princess**, North Promenade, would have first runs from Warners and Metro Goldwyn Mayer, whilst her opposite number, the **Hippodrome**, Church Street, regularly came down the scale a little and offered re-issues that were many and varied. Sunday nights specialised in 'H' (for horror) certificate films such as Universal's *Frankenstein* series or Warner's *Beast with Five Fingers* which sent the nervous scurrying home through gas lit streets.

Second feature coming up, and where better to see it than at that fine Edwardian leisure centre, the **Palace**, Bank Hey Street/Promenade. This magnificent building was eventually demolished and a liquorice allsorts box erected in its place. A Saturday evening at the Palace was entertainment at its very best. The building itself has had no expense spared; marble, glass and red plush abounded and commissionaires attired as Field Marshalls kept order. The Palace contained as ornate a ballroom as one could imagine, the perimeter balcony being supported by what I recollect were Greek gods and goddesses. Apart from ceiling lighting by means of crystal chandeliers, all

additional lighting was concealed under the ballroom
floor itself. All in all, the room had more the appearance of
Versailles than Blackpool Promenade and in the unlikely
event of *Francis Collins and his Rythamagicians* playing
a minuet instead of a foxtrot the atmosphere would have
been complete. A variety theatre was also contained in the
building. This was constructed and decorated in the best
traditions of gilt and red plush. Top line artistes appeared
weekly. In the best traditions of Blackpool adaptability, I
distinctly remember seeing Will Hay in *Oh Mr Porter* on a
Sunday night when the theatre was converted into a
cinema. Bars and cafes abounded without a ha'p'orth
of trouble. The piece-de-resistance however was the
cinema. *Grauman's Chinese* on Hollywood's Sunset Boule-
vard could not have been finer. In keeping with the rest of
the building the design was ornate without being overdone.
The pervading atmosphere was one of class. Larger than
life murals adored the walls of the side circle and the
wood panelling and brass fittings of the stalls could not be
bettered. Double feature programmes were regularly
shown at 2 p.m., 5 p.m., and 8 p.m., with one performance
at 7 p.m. on Sundays. Prices were from 2/- and for this the
nimble of foot could sample most of the first house
varieties, a quick step, a quick half and then into the
second house pictures. To my mind, the first crack in the
fabric of cinema-going appeared when the Palace handed
out cardboard spectacles and we were treated to a
three dimensional screening of Vincent Price in *The House
of Wax,* a remake of the 1933 Lionel Attwell thriller *The
Mystery of the Wax Museum.* Very entertaining as a
novelty but from then on it was downhill all the way.

As many of you like me, will be at times (chronologically
speaking) in second childhood when discussing cinema it
is perhaps appropriate to remember the Saturday morning and Saturday afternoon shows for children. The two
best remembered differed dramatically in both clientele
and programming. The morning shows at the **Odeon**,
Dickson Road, were a reasonably civilised affair with
orderly queuing at the side entrance in Springfield Road
and the seating being marshalled on a row-by-row basis by
staff and elder children.

Programmes were innocuous, although during the war
years, by means of propaganda films sometimes in the
form of singsongs we were encouraged to scream abuse at
Adolf and Musso-da-Wop. There would be the inevitable
serial in the managerial hope of keeping up attendances
for at least thirteen weeks. These ranged from *Don*

Winslow of the Navy to, best of them all, *Flash Gordon* whose exploits on the planet Mungo involving Ming the Merciless and other terrors has never been bettered. Feature films varied and hearts sank when an offering from the *Children's Film Foundation* appeared—we knew we were in for a very soppy hour and conversations started in the interval recommenced. On these occasions managers usually anticipated boredom setting in and put the serial on last thus ensuring a reasonable standard of behaviour until the end of the performance. I remember that on one occasion an unwary manager let slip through a showing of *Ghost Breakers* possibly because it starred the comedian Bob Hope. Whilst basically a comedy the film contained some quite frightening sequences set in an old mansion. This went down well with the young audience who were partial to a bit of horror, although many an elder sister was obliged to take younger brother for a quick visit to the toilet when things livened up on the screen far beyond the normal 'U' certificate fare. **The Empire**, Hawes Side Lane, Saturday afternoon tuppeny rush was a very different kettle of celluloid. For a start, the noise was deafening—and that was from the audience. Orange peel and apple cores rained down almost unabated and rest assured the Children's Film Foundation never had a look in—the manager knew his audience. Action was the order of the day and any more than ten seconds of continuous dialogue resulted in the hub-bub gradually increasing until the soundtrack was drowned, silence only resuming at the next gun shot. The over-rowdy were thrown out, but many regained entrance through the fire doors conveniently opened by pals. The end resulted in a mad rush up the aisles and out into the daylight where the exploits of the *Lone Ranger* and *Zorro* were re-enacted with great vigour. You had to have your wits about you when visiting the Empire—I think they now call it being street-wise.

I regret being unable to reminisce in detail about the many other Blackpool cinemas all of which had something distinctive about them. Sorry **Palladium**, Waterloo Road, **Alexandra** (or was it Alexander?), Manchester Square. Sorry, **Ritz** Chapel Street, **Tivoli**, Clifton Street, **Imperial**, Dickson Road, **Dominion**, Red Bank Road and **Oxford**, Waterloo Road.

BLACKPOOL'S T' BEST!   by Joan Pomfret

"There's nowt like Blackpool!" Missis Ogden allus sed to
me—
"Ther's fooaks 'at praises Foreign spots, an' rave ower
t'sun an't'sea!
They're nobbut being' snobbish-like, an' keepin' up wi'
t'rest
*O' **t'neighbours**! Tek no notice, love, fer Blackpool's allus*
t'Best!"

"Wheer else con yo' find miles o' sands an' piers an'
gradely fare?
An' t'Circus—aye, an't'Pleasure Beach—an' Shows
beyond compare?
An' landladies 'at knows ther' job, providin' 'Whoam fro'
whoam'
Yo'll nod find equalled onywheer, heawiver far yo' roam?"

"Ther's t'Teawr—an't'Winther Gardens—an' grand
Trams to tek yo' rides
To Fleetwood an' to Cleveleys, an' a score o' spots besides!
An' t'childer love them Donkey Rides an' Candy Floss,
an't'Fun—
Ah tell yo', Blackpool's got o' t' lot, summat fer everyone!"

"So dorn'd tek off to Palma, love, or Benidorm or France!
Just stick to Blackpool—**id**'s got Style an' Vigour an'
Romance!
An' think on—id's meant 'Holidays' fer mony an' mony a
year
*Fer gradely fooak like thee **an'** me an' t'rest o'*
Lancashire!"

BLACKPOOL   by Elsie Wallace

Ah went t' Blackpool t' other day
An' stopped to stare and ponder
O' t' days when we were nobbut kids,
Fro' t' valley o'er yonder.

We used t' cum 'ere every year,
Nobbut fer a day,
It were only folks as were well off
As could cum 'ere t' stay.

117

By gum, we 'ad a gradely time,
On t' sands bi t' Central Pier,
It cost us nowt except us fare,
An' all things 'appened 'ere.

There were big fat ladies paddlin',
Showin' all ther' knickers,
Sally Army singin' songs,
An' on t' prom "Stifkey's Vicar".

Owd fellas sittin' in ther' vests
We papers o'er ther faces,
Punch and Judy, donkey rides,
All t' folks fro' different places.

I' Chapel Street were t' smell o' chips,
At bottom, Fairyland,
To us it seemed like Paradise
T' live in a place so grand.

Ther' wer' t' th' organ grinder under t' bridge,
Big pies in t' cook-shop windus,
Sticks o' rock an' bags o' shrimps—
Nowt froze by Ross or Findus.

Ah've lived 'ere now nigh twenty years,
By gum, it's changed a lot—
The things Ah see round 'ere these days
Are now't but tommy rot.

There's bingo, pubs and clubs galore,
Gamblin', strip shows too,
If ther's nowt i' these t' interest thee,
What else con ti do?

Tha sits like me, i' thi little nest,
Thinkin' o' th' owd pleasures
An' 'ope as young uns cumin' up
Will 'ave memories they can treasure.

They'll not be 'alf as good as mine,
There's nowt left t' be done,
Except t' visit moon, er mars,
An' Ah can't think that's much fun.

Still, perhaps like me, when they get owd,
They'll stop an' think an' wonder,
At things they could and should 'ave done,
Way back when they were younger.

Off to Blackpool by "Billy Button" (R.H. Brodie) 1912.

We're gooin' off to Blackpool,
  An' lodgin' deawn South Shore;
There's miles o' sands an' donkeys,
  An' th' grand owd ocean's roar.

There's allus summat gooin' on,
  Brass melts reet fast deawn theer;
There's creawds on t'Prom when th' season's on,
  An' th' same on any Pier.

Yo' con have a sail an' catch some fluke,
  Or swagger on to th' Pier;
Yo' con tak a trip on th' ocean wave,
  When feelin' eawt o' gear.

For giddy folk that's fond o' life,
  There's th' South Shore Pleasure Beach;
There's th' Water Chute an' th' Switchback, too,
  Which makes aw th' women screech.

A gradely place is Blackpool,
  Plenty o' brine an' breeze;
There's lots o' sawt i'th' wayter,
  Yo' con sniff it at yo're ease.

If yo' want to dine there's plenty o' shops,
  Aw ready wi' dinners hot;
If yo' want a ride to Singleton,
  There's landaus theer on't spot.

If you're feelin' bad, an' want a rest,
  Pack up yo're traps an' come,
Bring plenty o' brass, or else by the Mass,
  You'd better stop awhum.

EH, BILL! COME TO BLACKPOOL
by Langford Saunders

Eh, Bill, come to Blackpool! an' bring thie wife, Mary,
Hoo looks fairly run deawn wi' toilin' through t'day;
An' bring Jack an' Nelly—that curly-nobbed fairy—
That cowf ut hoo's getten ull soon pass away.
It's lively just neaw—for there's crowds o' folk walkin'
Up an' deawn th' Promenade fro' mornin' till neet;
They're as happy as con be, lowfin' an' tawkin'—
By gum, Blackpool just neaw's a raily grand seet!

Come on to Blackpool—yo' may spend a nice hower
In a sail fro' th' North Pier to Fleetwood an' back;
Or a grand afternoon i' roamin' through th' Tower,
For th' monkeys an' tigers ull please yore Jack.
Yo' may goo on to th' piers—there's skatin' an dancin',
Or ride to th' South Shore, an' get fun eaut o' th' fair;
Or tak' childer on t' sands, an' jine i' their prancin,
An' help um build castles—theau's built some i' th' air!

Get ready; come neaw! for I've getten a notion
Ut a sniff o' th' briny ull do yo aw good;
An' breathin' th' ozone fro' th' owd rollickin' ocean
Is th' reet soart o' physic to tingle one's blood.
Yo want'en a change— maybe Fayther Time's markin'
A notch in his stick as each yer ebbs away;
So pack up thi luggage, tha connot keep warkin'—
If Tha o'erdraws Natur, tha'll have to repay.

So come on to Blackpool, yo'll never repent it,
It's rare bracin' place for owd folk an' young,
This invite's i' good faith, tha'll be glad as I sent it,
It's a good salve for dumps to mix up wi' t'thrung.
It's a lovely sayside for rest or for pleasure,
Wi' th' waves rowlin' high or just lavin' one's feet;
Yo' may strowl upo' th' cliffs—get health without
*   measure,*
So come, an' durnt miss such a glorious treat.

BLACKPOOL
by Tom Platts

There's a town in the West where King Pleasure holds
  sway—
An ideal resort for a real holiday—
Where health-giving ozone is borne on the breeze
Which sweeps o'er the surface of wide-spreading seas.
From its shores proudly rise stately halls of romance,
Whose magical splendours the senses entrance,
Where the wonders of Fairyland dazzle the eyes,
And in song, dance, and revel Time merrily flies.
On golden-hued sands there the tripper may roam,
And children may dabble with glee in the foam.
From office, and workshop, and schoolroom set free,
They give themselves up to the spell of the sea—
Ever-changing in mood, yet each change full of charm—
Now swirling in tempest, now placid and calm;
Now rippling with joy in the sun's cheerful glow,
Or sighing, or sobbing, in ebb or in flow.
Would you like to enjoy its alluring delights,
And view for yourselves its sensational sights?
Be Health, Relaxation, or Pleasure your quest?
Hie forth, then, to Blackpool—this town in the West.

Tom Platts was a printer and a Socialist who was one of
those involved in the setting up of Blackpool Union
Printers in 1892. He wrote a poem (c.1913) called *Spare
The Gynn* in an effort to stop developers knocking down
that old pub.

THE BLACKPOOL CARNIVAL SONG 1923
Words and music by Harry Lowther

There is a place where at night or in day—time
You're al—ways sure of a merry and gay time
Jo—li—ty round you when—ev—er you're there.
Car—ni—val! Car—ni—val! ev—e—ry-where!
You've been! You must have been! You know the place
I mean.....

Chorus

Black—pool Black—pool Oh, what a gay "there and back"
pool!
Eh, my word, it's a grand pool! What pool? BLACK POOL!
Dai—ly gai—ly dancing be—side the sea.
Al—ways play—time, Hip, hip, hur—ray time!
Black—pool's the place for me!

Sing, loud—ly sing till we rend ev—ery raft—er
Fa—ces a—glow, and our hearts full of laugh—ter,
Sea—scent—ed breezes! There's life in the air!
Mu—sic and Ma—gic! The world is a fair!
In cho—rus let it go.....Hel—lo! Hel—lo! Hel—lo!

SOME BLACKPOOL SHIPWRECKS
By Kenneth Price

For years afterwards Blackpool folk talked about the day when a ship crashed into North Pier and sent four shops tumbling into the sea.

Local boatmen kept a wary look-out on that eventful morning of Sunday, October 9, 1892, as hurricane winds sent giant waves thundering against the promenade.

Then between ten and eleven o'clock they saw her—the 667-ton Norwegian barque *Sirene* floundering helplessly. It did not take a seaman's practised eye to see that the crew had lost all control as their vessel drifted drunkenly towards the land.

Like lightning the news spread swiftly through the town and thousands of residents, indifferent to crashing waves and drenching spray, crowded onto the seafront to watch the unfolding drama.

They all expected the stricken ship to grind ashore between Central and North Piers; if she had her crew would almost certainly have perished, for in that cauldron of inshore waves no rescue boat would survive.

Instead, the *Sirene* began to lurch towards the North Pier, from which dozens of terrified spectators now bolted with all the speed of athletic runners to the safety of the Promenade.

On she came, remorseless and menacing, now wallowing fore to aft, now swaying from port to starboard and back again—on, on and on, until with a fearful crash she ploughed into the pier and shuddered back.

Her captain, in spite of the apparently insuperable odds against him, had decided that their best hope of survival lay in trying to reach the pier....he judged rightly. The initial impact brought the ship's deck roughly level with the pier, enabling him and his crew of eleven to leap onto the pier helped by lifeboatmen and other willing Blackpool citizens.

Danger soon confronted the rescuers, however, as the ship frenziedly struck the pier while they hauled the sailors to safety....as the last crewman came off the vessel struck again dislodging part of the pier on which rescuers had stood only moments before.

Again the ship thrust forward, slicing into the pier to demolish several supports and send four smashed shops tumbling into the sea.

But no lives had been lost—that was the main thing.

A few years earlier, another Norwegian ship, the *Abana*, provided Blackpool with another drama of the sea. The 1,269-ton barque was sailing in ballast for the United States when hurricane-force winds ripped her sails to shreds and tangled her rigging in knots.

All seemed hopeless....until Captain Danielsen spotted a light on the cliffs. The Norwegians, thinking it was a lighthouse, steered towards it; actually it was a beacon lit by Doctor Hardman of Bispham.

Meanwhile, Blackpool lifeboat was carried on a horse-drawn cart from the town centre to Bispham, where its crew were soon pulling on their oars towards the stranded Abana which was now gradually breaking up under the pounding waves 150 yards offshore.

"How many can you take?" shouted Captain Danielsen, as the rescue craft approached. "There are seventeen of us."

"We'll take you all," lifeboat coxswain Cartmell yelled back. Into the lifeboat the Norwegians crammed themselves; and now, with thirty-three people on board, Mr Cartmell steered for the shore.

Once the overloaded lifeboat stuck on a sandbank only to be released by a lifeboatman who jumped into the boiling sea to push his boat clear.

The rescued mariners were taken to the Red Lion Hotel, Bispham, feted by the villagers and given Christmas dinner and tea. An unusual Christmas for the villagers and now only a memory...but you can still see the ribs of the Abana on the sands off Little Bispham.

Blackpool's most celebrated shipwreck was that of the Foudroyant, one of the wooden walls of England and for a time flagship of the great Admiral Nelson himself.

Launched in 1798, the 80-gun ship of 2,055 tons saw service in the Napoleonic wars after which she was laid up before becoming an instruction ship. Reports in 1891 of plans to break her up provoked an outcry, one protester being Sir Arthur Conan Doyle, author of the Sherlock Holmes stories, who wrote a poem about it.

The Foudroyant was saved from the breaker's yard by Mr G.W. Cobb, of Caldicott Castle, near Chepstow, who bought the ship for £6,000 and restored and refitted her at a cost of £20,000. His decision to exhibit her at seaside resorts brought the old warship to Blackpool in June 1897.

It was a great attraction; local boatmen did a brisk trade taking people out to see her at her offshore moorings and on June 15th a dance was held on board.

A fierce gale blew up early next morning, Foudroyant dragged her anchors and began drifting inshore with gathering speed. The crew of twenty-eight men and boys were unable to help themselves as their doomed ship lurched perilously forward, barely missing North Pier... drifting towards the Hotel Metropole.

On she went until with a grinding noise she beached and heeled over. Her sailors were all safely landed and taken to the Wellington Hotel for a dry-down and a welcome meal.

The Foudroyant had cheated the shipbreakers only to end up a wreck on Blackpool beach. The wreck was sold to a firm which did what the breakers would have done; the ship's metal parts were fashioned into all sorts of objects like plaques and ash trays; furniture and fittings were made from some of the salvaged timber.

Like the campaign for her preservation, the inglorious end of the Foudroyant inspired verse. It was, however, less noble than the poem Conan Doyle wrote a few years before.

It appeared in the window of a Blackpool shop selling souvenirs of the wreck, and read simply:

The glorious decks Nelson strode
Are now on sale in Talbot road.

Blackpool's Pleasure Steamers at the turn of the Century

Name	When Built	Where Built	Tonnage	Owner
Greyhound	1895	Cylde	211	North Pier Steamship Co
Queen of the North	1895	Birkenhead	242	Blackpool Passenger Steamboat Co
Belle	1892	Plymouth	55	North Pier Steamship Co
Bickerstaffe	1879	Birkenhead	97	Blackpool Passenger Steamboat Co
Clifton	1871	Preston	34	North Pier Steamship Co
Wellington	1872	Preston	53	Blackpool Passenger Steamboat Co
Roses	1876	Rutherglen	55	Morecambe Steamboat Co
Express	1892	Kinghorn	88	Morecambe Steamboat Co

SAILING BOATS AT THE TURN OF THE CENTURY
by Bob Dobson

A few years ago, there came into my hands a document which has a tale to tell. It bears the official stamp of the Chief Constable's Office, July 1899 and shows a drawing of the Promenade from the Metropole Hotel to the Wellington Hotel at Central Pier. On the landward side, various landmarks are shown: The Tower, The Alhambra, Lane Ends, Heywood Street (that's still there—it just wants finding, you've walked past it thousands of times). The sands are divided into 3 areas, showing that in that space may be 5, 8 or 4 sailing boats. The area south of Central Pier is marked "May be used by No. 1 if they so desire". I interpret the document as being one which shows which boatkeepers are licensed by the Corporation to stand their boats there. In those days, the Borough Police would deal with matters such as boat licences. It ensured some order on the sands. However, for me the interesting aspect of the document is the names of the boatmen. All are from families long, and still, associated with the sea and the life-boats. I list them:-

Group 1
Jas. Barrow, 11 Middle Street; Benjamin Caton, Exchange Street; John Eccleston, 8 Eden Street; Thomas Hayes, 8 Upper Talbot Street; Peter Lowe, 4 Eden Street; James Rimmer, 9 Wellington Street; Robert Sutton, Erdington Road; Thomas Singleton, 25 Queens Road; Anthony Salthouse, 21 Elizabeth Street.

Group 2
John Cartmell, 23 Oddfellow Street; Cuthbert Cornall, 3 Cragg Street; John Cornall, 15 Chapel Street; William Parr, 11 Yorkshire Street; Frank Parr, 12 Wellington Street; John Richard Parr, 2 Yorkshire Street; Richard Parr, 3 Bickerstaffe Street; Samuel Rimmer, 10 Wellington Street; James Rimmer, 10 Chapel Street; William Stanhope, 26 Bonny Street.

Group 3
Thomas Bilsborough, 6 Hyde Road; Richard Cornall, Wellington Street; Robert Parkinson, 12 Bolton Street; Robert I. Scott, 11 Back Oddfellow Street; Richard Westhead, 14 Moon Street.

BLACKPOOL'S LIFESAVING HEROES by David Pearce

Long before there were any lifeboats on the Fylde Coast, many heroic rescues of life at sea had been achieved locally.

After all, sailors had been crossing the waters of Morecambe Bay for centuries—back to the Romans and beyond. It's not a rocky shore but it can be a very dangerous one. When howling gales roared in from some quarter of the west, a sailing ship master could find himself unable to make headway against the storm. Then he would be forced closer and closer to the land. His battered ship would find herself in the shallow waters filled with sandbanks just off the coast and run aground. Then the breakers, rolling in under the relentless wind, would smash the ship to matchwood. If the crew tried to swim to safety they were drowned. Only a skilful boatman had a hope in hell of saving them from this maritime inferno.

North Bank, North Wharf, Horse Bank, Salthouse Bank.. they were graveyards for many a fine ship although the cargoes of cloth, alcohol and foodstuffs were sometimes more than welcome booty on the beach for the few hardy souls who eked a living on the Fylde coast 200 and more years ago.

And so the catalogue of disaster went on as the town of Blackpool began to grow into a holiday resort in the mid 1800's.

Fishing was an important local activity then and its leading figure was Bob Bickerstaffe who was usually to the fore in any rescue attempt.

On a moonlit November night in 1862 he swam out to a wreck opposite where the Imperial Hotel stands. Bob trailed a rope with him and all but one of the crew of the schooner *Ada* were rescued although Bob was thought to be dead when he was dragged onshore again!

After the formation of the Royal National Lifeboat Institution in 1824, Lytham had been provided with a lifeboat in 1851.

Just eight years later, Fleetwood became a lifeboat station. And, in 1864, Blackpool joined the ranks. For two years, local worthies had been raising funds after several generous gifts of cash set the ball rolling. The idea of providing a Blackpool lifeboat was not a new one. Thirty years before, the Reverend William Thornber, Vicar of St John's, Blackpool, who wrote the definitive history of the place, was advocating one.

The *Robert William* was launched on July 14, 1864 with Bob Bickerstaffe as coxswain. Members of the Parr and Stanhope families who kept their links with Blackpool RNLI through to modern times, were in the crew.

The first service rendered assistance to a brig in difficulties during bad weather. The *St Michael of Le Havre* went on her way to Fleetwood on a wild Sunday morning in September that year.

In his report, Bob Bickerstaffe noted that the *Robert William*, "Rowed well and, under sail, went like a steamer."

Many lifeboat crews in those far off days were largely made up of fishermen so poor that they were glad of the few shillings they could earn from a service. But competition for a lifebelt in the Blackpool boat was razor keen for the honour it afforded. The tale is told of a crewman in 1865 who arrived late for a service and offered a sovereign for a place at the oars!

On April 11, 1867, the lifeboatmen went to three wrecks in a day. First they waded into the surf near Central Pier to help ashore four men from a small vessel driven ashore there. Then they launched to a ship in difficulties, put a man onboard to assist and let Lytham lifeboat get the ship to safer waters in the Ribble. Meanwhile, the Blackpool boat went on to a third wreck and saved all 14 onboard—the first of 130 souls who owed their lives to the skill and determination of Blackpool lifeboatmen.

Not all shipwrecked mariners were so lucky as the men of the *Susan L. Campbell.*

When the brig *Favourite* of Liverpool ran aground off Cleveleys one wild November night, in 1865, Bob Bickerstaffe and his men battled for two hours to get alongside the wreck but were beaten back by the storm. The rudder of the lifeboat was damaged and 10 oars smashed by the fury of the sea and in the end, their efforts were in vain. The little ship capsized and sank and her crew were drowned—just a few miles from their home port with a cargo of nuts and palm oil from West Africa.

Probably the most famous rescue by the *Robert William* was the case of the *Bessie Jones* in February, 1880. The Fleetwood schooner was nearly home with a cargo of steel rails when she was wrecked on the Salthouse Bank between South Shore and St Annes. There was a north west gale and it was bitterly cold with showers of hail as the lifeboat battled her way out to the wreck. One of the crew of five had already been swept to his death from the schooner and the rest were lashed to the rigging as great seas surged over the stricken vessel. It took two hours to manoeuvre the boat into position with an anchor down so that she could be veered down onto the schooner and the crew rescued. With them safely onboard, Coxswain Bickerstaffe set off for the nearest safe beach—at St Annes. But on the way a giant wave almost turned the little craft over. Lifeboatmen and survivors were thrown into the bottom of the boat and crewman Jack Fish went overboard. As he clung on for dear life, another sea swept over them all and only then could he be dragged back on board.

Blackpool got a new lifeboat in September 1885. The *Samuel Fletcher* was launched with great ceremony on the day that Blackpool's famous trams were unveiled for the first time.

The following year saw the *Mexico* disaster when lifeboatmen from Southport and St Annes lost their lives and the Lytham boat rescued the crew of the ill fated German ship in the Ribble estuary. Blackpool lifeboat was called out to search for the overdue St Annes boat.

Three days before Christmas, 1894, the lifeboat had to be dragged by horses through country lanes to be launched at Bispham where the *Abana* had grounded. All 17 on board were saved.

The *Samuel Fletcher* figured in the rescue of the crew from Nelson's old ship the *Foudroyant* which ran aground near North Pier in 1897. Now, that old lifeboat still sails on the more peaceful waters of the lake in Blackpool's lovely Stanley Park.

It was the era of the sailing ship and the sailing lifeboat that loomed large in the proud history of lifesaving at Blackpool.

After the turn of the century, the station was equipped with motor lifeboats but never saw any service as dramatic or spectacular as those early days.

In more recent years, the Royal National Lifeboat Institution decided that a conventional lifeboat was not needed at the resort. Instead, they believed that small inshore rescue craft could handle the problems caused when swimmers got into difficulties on the busy beaches. But local lifeboatmen do not believe this to be the case and have campaigned for a bigger boat to once again be stationed at Blackpool. They have raised hundreds of thousands of pounds in a fund to pay for it but the RNLI has nothing suitable for the task. Major offshore duties are left these days to Fleetwood and Lytham stations.

THE FOUDROYANT   by Bob Dobson

First launched in 1789, and named after a French flag-ship captured in the mid-18th century, this fine 90-gun ship was to be a flagship for many admirals of the British Navy, including Lord Nelson in 1799 and 1800. She was on active service until 1812. By 1892 she was in need of restoration, and a Mr Cobb bought her then for £6,000 and had her completely re-rigged and fitted out from the original Admiralty plans. In 1897 he was sailing her with a crew of 6 and some boys taken on for training around the British coastal resorts.

On 16th June 1897, whilst moored 2 miles off Blackpool, a terrible storm arose. The ship broke her cable and was blown ashore near North Pier. The story of that six-hour storm and the terrible damage to the lady of the sea is told in a letter Cobb wrote to his mother from the safety of the Wellington Hotel the following day. It is preserved in Caldicot Castle along with a large cannon and the figurehead representing Mars, the God of War. Let's read parts of it........

We went back to the ship yesterday and her condition was horrifying...the huge old timbers are torn and ripped in every direction, every internal fitting and bulk head swept away and the decks torn up and rent to pieces....The violence with which she bumped and the weight of the seas which swept her is shown by several of the lower deck guns having ploughed grooves about 3 feet deep through the sills and the solid oak sides. The one bright feature, though it doubles my pain, was the behaviour of the boys, which could not have been finer ......For six hours they were cold and hungry and drenched to the skin, the ship striking heavily every minute or two and gradually going to pieces under the great seas which swept her, but they never murmured or showed a sign of fear...Then we all sheltered under the poop, keeping clear of the wheel which spun round dangerously every time the rudder struck...The boys sang "Hearts of Oak" and "The Death of Nelson", and all were in good spirits though no one in his heart could have seen much hope. The upper masts were bending like whips and the first to go was the fore t'gallant and the main soon followed.... All the chairs and loose furniture had smashed down in a heap to leeward and everyone had to hold on by ring- bolts or ropes....Water began to come in everywhere, and at last the stern bulkhead opened boldly like a

*door and a great sea rushed in....Just before the fore-
mast and bowsprit had broken off short and gone over
the side, the whole poop had gone visibly over to leeward, and I felt that, being new work, it could not stand
and we should be crushed under it, so we all clambered
on top of it so that when it went we should have a chance
of jumping overboard. It would not have made much
difference, as no one could have lived two minutes in
the sea....I never saw (waves) half so big as they were,
all rough and broken. Now we saw the main mast break
short and go over....The boys were so completely
drenched and exhausted that it wasn't safe to stay
where we were, as they would have been washed over,
so we went back under the poop and risked being
crushed. We were sheltered there and wedged ourselves
together to get a little warmth. The boys revived and
sweet-voiced Colby started "Eternal Father strong to
save" which we all took up....Just in front, through a
hatch-way, we could look down into the main deck,
nearly full up with water, while further the quarter-
deck was bulging and splitting, and the stump of the
main-mast bumping up and down....one almost wished
the next wave would do the work and finish us....*

Thousands of people flocked onto the sands after the
storm abated to look for souvenirs. The Glasgow company
Cobb contracted with to salvage the wreck recovered some
of their expense by selling the remains, from which
articles were fashioned and sold to tourists. Some of these
relics of a sad event in Blackpool's history remain still
in the town, treasured by descendants of those who had
witnessed the sea's work that wild night.

5.   Fact & Fiction

Some impressions of Blackpool as a Holiday Resort

Here is a full display of beauty and fashion. Here the eye faithful to its trust, conveys intelligence from the heart of one sex to that of the other; gentle tumults rise in the breast; intercourse opens in tender language; the softer passions are called into action; Hymen approaches, kindles his torch and cements that union which continues for life. Here may be seen folly flushed with money, shoe-strings, and a phaeton and four. Keen envy sparkles in the eye at the display of a new bonnet. The heiress of eighteen trimmed in black, and a hundred thousand pounds, plentifully squanders her looks of disdain, or the stale belle, who has outstood her market, offers her fading charms upon easy terms.
From William Hutton's *A Description of Blackpool in 1788* (Blackpool's first Guide Book).

★   ★   ★   ★   ★

You desire an account of Blackpool. You shall have it. Blackpool is situated on a level dreary moorish coast; the cliffs are of earth and not very high. It consists of a few houses ranged in line with the sea and four of these are for the reception of company. One accommodates 30, one 60, one 80 and the other 100 persons. We were strangers to all, and on the recommendation of the master of the inn at Preston we drove to the house of 80 which is called Lane's End. The company now conisted of about 70 and I never found myself in such a mob. The people sat down to table behind their knives and forks to be ready for their dinner, while my mother, my father and myself, who did not choose to scramble, stood behind till someone more considerate than the rest made room for us. These people are, in general, of a species called Boltoners, that is rich, rough, honest manufacturers of the town of Bolton, whose coarseness of manners is proverbial even amongst their countrymen. The other houses are frequented by better

*company, that is Lancashire gentry, Liverpool merchants
and Manchester manufacturers. I find here that I have no
equals but the lawyers, for those who are my equals in
fortune are distinguished by their vulgarity, and those who
are my equals in manners are above me in situation.
Fortunately for me, there is no lack of lawyers in
Lancashire. Preston alone containing 50, and there are
always at Blackpool some whom I like, and with these I
laugh at the rest.*

(Catherine Hutton 1788)

★　★　★　★　★

*At a distance of five miles west of Poulton is Blackpool,
which within the last thirty years has attained some
distinction as a watering place. For this purpose its
situation and other characteristics are peculiarly favour-
able, whether we consider its fine breezes from the
western ocean, its flat and smooth beach, to the breadth of
half-a-mile when the tide is out, the straight coast for
nearly twenty miles, or the purity of the water with which
its visitors are supplied. The name is derived from a pool
of water of a black, dark or liver colour, which formerly
was known to be at its south end, but now filled up and
converted into meadow ground. Some faint views of the
Isle of Man to the north-west may be seen from the land
behind it on a clear evening; to the north the fells of
Westmoreland at forty miles distance, the crags of
Lancashire, and the hills of Cumberland are visible; to the
south, even at fifty miles distance, are seen the mountains
of North Wales; but the rising ground to the east limits the
prospect on that side. Such is the situation of Blackpool.
The sea has encroached upon the land here very
considerably within the memory of persons now living,
and, from the flatness of the beach, no vessel can approach
the shore, and even the smallest boat cannot be entered
without wading. The tradition of the country is that a
public house stood upon the firm sand, near a stone called
Penny-Stone, which is now at least half-a-mile from the
shore. The sea, probably from its little depth, affords but
few fish; though freshwater fish and those of a mixed
nature are abundant from the rivers Lune, Wyre and
Ribble. Near the south end of the hamlet is a building
called Vauxhall (Foxhall), now in a state of ruinous decay.
It was long the retreat of Popish recusants, and in 1715
was fitted up to receive the Pretender, in a state of con-
cealment, till matters were ripe for a general insurrection,*

*and being surrounded by a lofty wall, it was only
accessible from the north, the south and east sides being
defended by a pool and a swamp, and on the sea side
could not be approached by any vessel. It also contained
many secret recesses and hiding places, and was therefore
well adapted to guard against surprise. The regulations for
bathing at Blackpool are certainly entitled to approbation.
At the proper time of the tide a bell rings for the ladies
to assemble, when no gentlemen must be seen on the
parade, under forfeiture of a bottle of wine; and on their
retiring, the bell again rings to summon the gentlemen to a
similar ceremony. On the sea beach is the parade, a
pleasant grass walk of about six yards wide, by 200 yards
in length. A news-house and coffee-room have been
established here for the convenience of visitors, who, in
some seasons, have amounted to 400 or more.*

(From: *The Beauties of England and Wales.* Britton 1807.)

*No sea-bathing place can be better situated (than
Blackpool)—opening out to the sea, refreshed with a pure
and bracing air, presenting a fine, smooth sand, new-
modelled by every tide, but always firm, safe and elastic,
and furnished with excellent accommodations.*

*No wonder will be felt that there are here frequently at
the height of the season from eight hundred to a thousand
visitors (at the time Blackpool's population was 750).
Blackpool has always been frequented by persons of rank
fashion, of whom there are many to be found here in the
summer months, mixed with good company from the
manufacturing districts.*

*The houses of public reception are scattered along the
coast with an aspect to the Irish Sea, and in the rear
are the habitations of the villagers ....*

*On the verge of the sea, fenced from its precipitous
banks by a white railing, is the parade, where the valetud-
inarian inhales the sea air in perfection, and those who
resort to Blackpool not only to seek health but to enjoy and
preserve it, find this a very agreeable promenade.*

(Edward Baines History of Lancashire. 1824.)

BLACKPOOL IN 1830

In 1830 was published Clarke's *New Lancashire Gazetteer*. It listed all the towns, villages and hamlets of the county. Here is what is said about the places now in the borough. You will quickly perceive that there has been some— what's the word—progress (?)

Blackpool, a hamlet in the township of Layton with Warbreck, parish of Bispham, hundred of Amounderness, 18 miles W. from Preston. Blackpool owes its name to a bed of dark peaty water at the south of the town; but which, from draining, has nearly disappeared; near this pool was an ancient mansion, surrounded by a wall and now in decay, called Fox Hall, belonging to the Tildesley family, which Sir Thomas Tildesley fitted up to receive the Pretender in the year 1715, but which personage did not arrive in this part of the United Kingdom. From an obscure village, Blackpool has become a fashionable bathing-place: a most lively and pleasant sketch of it was writtten by the late Mr Hutton of Birmingham in the year 1788, since which the accommodations have considerably increased both in extent and price. The sea coast here forms a straight line for many miles; the bank or cliff, which is clay, rises to various heights from three to sixty feet above high-water mark, but great encroachments have been made on the shore. A stone in the sea, about half a mile distant, is said to mark the spot where a public house stood some ages back; to this iron hooks were fixed, to which travellers used to fasten their horses while they drank their penny pots of beer; whence the stone first acquired the name of Penny Stone: at present it is nearly covered with sea weed. The ocean at low water retreats half a mile from the shore, leaving a bed of solid sand, excellently well adapted for a ride or a drive to an extent of twenty miles. The time of bathing is nearly at the flood: a bell rings as a signal for the ladies; and, if a gentleman is seen on the parade before they retire, he forfeits a bottle of wine; when the female mysteries are concluded, the bell again rings for the gentlemen. The views from Blackpool are extensive, comprehending to the north the lofty fells of Furness and Cumberland, and to the south the picturesque mountains of North Wales. Some parts of the Isle of Man are also discoverable. Fish is scarce, though shrimps are plentiful; fishing is consequently not one of the pleasures of Blackpool, and sea excursions are little known, as, from the flatness of the sand, no vessel can approach the shore, nor can even the smallest boat be entered without wading. The tide rises from twelve to sixteen feet. The air is peculiarly pure and healthy, and the inhabitants remarkable for their longevity. Whilst a man lay expiring upon his bed, attended by his sympathizing friends, one of them, a woman, exclaimed, "Poor John, I knew him a clever young fellow fourscore years ago". Blackpool is much frequented by the nobility and gentry as well as by the manufacturers of the county. An Episcopa Chapel was consecrated a few years since. Here is also a building sometimes used as a barn, at other times as a theatre; and at Blackpool are found the usual concomitants of a place of fashionable resort, such as an assembly room, a news room, a library and coffee rooms. On the verge of the cliff and defended by a railing is the parade, a delightful promenade, much resorted to, which presents a commanding view of the ever fluctuating ocean, "on the surface of which", says Mr Hutton, "flow intelligence and commerce, whilst at its bottom lie immense riches; here the merchant finds wealth, the mariner too often a grave".

Bispham, a parish and township with Norbreck, in the hundred of Amounderness, 2 miles W. from Poulton in the Fylde. Inhabitants 323. A perpetual curacy in the archdeaconry of Chester. Patron P. Hesketh, esq. A mile to the north is the small hamlet of Little Bispham. This place was formerly called Biscopham, as pertaining to the archbishop of York, before the conquest. The church, recently rebuilt, contains an ancient Norman doorway. In the parish are two townships.   **Inhabitants**

	Inhabitants
Layton with Warbreck	749
Bispham with Norbreck	323
Entire population	1,072

Marton, Great, a chapelry in the parish of Poulton, hundred of Amounderness, 8 miles W. from Kirkham. Inhabitants 1397. Patron J. Clifton, esq., and others. Near this township is a small lake called Marton Mere, and also the somewhat extensive morass of Marton Moss.

Marton, Little, a hamlet in the preceding township.

Warbreck, a township with Layton in the parish of Bispham, hundred of Amounderness, 2½ miles W.S.W. from Poulton. Inhabitants 749.

Layton, a township with Warbreck, in the parish of Bispham, hundred of Amounderness, 2½ miles S.W. from Poulton in the Fylde. Rakes Hall, in this township, is the seat of John Hornby, esq.

★　★　★　★　★

*There are two great rival houses, in Blackpool,
Nixon's and Dickson's—the Capulets and the Montagues—
the white and the red rose. The former boasts of a
larger and more extended building, conspicuously white
from recent painting; the latter of a more projecting
cliff over the strand, and a private terrace with
greensward and neat rustic seats, quite still and retired,
though fronting the sea. This last hotel is frequented
chiefly by the higher class of visitors. At Nixon's the
company is less select—or rather it is of a lower grade
altogether.*

*Arrived at Nixon's in the very nick of time for dinner
and the necessary permission having been obtained on my
behalf and that of my travelling companion, we were
admitted into a long and lofty apartment having some
pretensions to the rank of a banqueting-room, in which a
long narrow table, groaning under a double line of tin-
capped dishes, was waiting the arrival of the company. A
loud-sounding scavenger-like bell soon brought the latter,
mob-fashion, into the room; when I took my place at the
bottom of the table, near to my coach companion, who,
having always been a guest at Dickson's or 'the upper
house', sat himself down here to oblige me, not without
symptoms of a curling lip and a turned-up nose.*

*Such a motley of honest-looking people—men, women
and children (for there were some whose chins did not
reach the edge of the table)—it has never been my fortune
to meet under the like circumstances in such numbers
before—fifty or sixty in all—except at the anniversary
dinner at some dispensary.*

*Methinks the highest in rank here might have been an
iron-founder from near Bradford or Halifax, or a retired
wine merchant, from Liverpool, who, in the palmy days of
Port, found the Oporto trade a thriving concern. About a
dozen chamber-maids acted as waiters, and there was
not a vestige of man-servant, at which I heartily rejoiced.
It fell to my lot to dissect the chickens for the ladies.
Abundance of meat and sauce seemed to be the desirable
thing. One whom I had plentifully supplied with leg and
pinion, and no small portion of the parsley and butter,
sent soon after to crave for the breast, and a little more
of the green sauce! The thing was appalling; and the
serious and busy manner in which every hand and mouth
seemed to be at work during the first ten minutes, sans
mot dire, plainly showed how palatable was the fare, and
how keenly the sea-air and sea-bathing of Blackpool, had
prepared the company for it.*

138

At Dickson's the scene is said to be somewhat more decorous and stately; for there the consuming classes, like the articles to be consumed, are of a different and a better order, although the charge at each place differs only by sixpence; five shillings being the highest price for not fewer than five meals a day.

(A.B. Granville 1839)

★   ★   ★   ★   ★

Numerous are the expedients resorted to by lodging-house keepers, during the bathing season, to fit up as many beds, and apologies for beds, as practicable, in the least possible space. Every available piece of furniture is converted, by the aid of certain ingenious appendages, into either a French, Tudor or tent bedstead. Drawers are often metamorphosised into dormitories, and we have heard a man assert that he had taken up his lodgings in a clock case, but that didn't exactly go down; yet there were many who can bear testimony to having, when no other accommodation offered, been happy to gain a night's rest in a bathing machine; and an unfortunate bedless fellow once eagerly enquired if he could not be accommodated with a pole, thrust through a bedroom window, upon which he could perch until morning. Beds are improvised in drawing rooms, kitchens, sculleries, and even cellars; aye and weary town-emancipated mortals have often been glad to pay high prices for common shakedowns in dreary outhouses, upon which to stretch their weary limbs and court repose.

A question most difficult of solution is, where do these lodging-house keepers themselves sleep during the summer season? Do they sleep at all? At every conceivable hour, night and day, they are on the alert, and if ever they court

'Nature's sweet restorer, balmy sleep,'

it must be on a perch up some unused chimney. In one department they are wonderful adepts—charging; but this is somewhat pardonable, as they have little more than four months of a harvest in which to reap supplies for the whole twelve. No wonder they glean so closely, and endeavour to 'make hay while the sun shines'—no wonder they keep such thieving cats, or that joints so rapidly absorb when taken from the table—that tea and sugar fail to last the allotted period, and that a shilling is charged for the intrinsic value of two-pennyworth. Lodgers at the

139

seaside are invariably considered the sheep that may be legitimately fleeced with impunity. Yet still poor deluded creatures will flock in crowds to wander 'by the sad sea waves,' and briefly sojourn where they are compelled to live uncomfortably, and put up with every conceivable inconvenience; and yet, by some strange freak of imagination, fancy they are enjoying themselves, and improving health and appetite—two things which in many cases, goodness knows, need no improvement.

(From *The Visit of Mr and Mrs Jeremiah Grubb and Family to Blackpool* by D. Longworth 1865.)

★   ★   ★   ★   ★

When I got down to the beach it was nearly high water, and the sight was, indeed, most exhilarating: the shore so gradually and gently that there is little danger in dipping, even for those who have not the stout arm of the strong swimmer, and as there is a plentiful supply of capital machines, with very civil attendants, the visitors have all the means and appliances for indulging in a tête a tête with any Triton that may happen to get so far north....Not caring about a bath on the day of my arrival, I rambled along the shore, enjoying the many amusing incidents arising from the induction of the uninitiated to an element, which numbers, I found, never had had the privilege of gazing at before. There was a gloriously high tide, accompanied with what one of the waggish boatmen styled a stiffish breeze, so that (to be naughtily nautical in my description) it was somewhat difficult, even for those who were scudding under bare poles, to avoid being laid upon their beam ends; but the bathers bore their tumbles evidently with great good humour, whilst the lookers-on, of course, laughed heartily when an unlucky wight got the benefit of a more than usually boisterous breaker, and was regularly swamped......

When the tide receded, there remained a long continuous range of beautiful hard smooth sand, on which there was every possible description of amusement usually found at watering places. There were hosts of embryo candidates for the diggings, not auriferous—cricketers of every caste and calibre, save those seen at Lord's—target shooters, innocent of any inheritance from the apple-hitting hero of Switzerland,—and for equestrian performances, ponies possessing every pie-bald and

140

picturesque peculiarity of conformation that freakish nature, in her most facetious moments, ever manufactured,— whilst, lastly, tho' not the least of the attractions to the lovers of fun, there was a troop of donkeys that would have done credit to the cockneyfied haunts of Hampstead or Blackheath.
(From *Studies About Blackpool, the Brighton of the North.* Pencillings from the portfolio of Peter Pastil. (1868))

★   ★   ★   ★   ★

NORBRECK

At the western edge of that quiet tract of Lancashire called the Fylde, lying between Wyre, Ribble and the Irish Channel, the little wind-swept hamlet of Norbreck stands, half asleep, on the brow of a green ridge overlooking the sea. The windows of a white-washed cottage wink over its garden wall as the traveller comes up the slope, between tall hedgerows; and very likely he will find all so still that, but for wild birds that crowd the air with music, he could hear his footsteps ring on the road as clearly as if he were walking on the flags of a gentleman's greenhouse. In summer, when its buildings are glittering in their annual suit of new whitewash, and when all the country round looks green and glad, it is a pleasant spot to set eyes upon, —this quiet hamlet overlooking the sea. At that time of year it smells of roses, and of cribs were oxen lie and the little place is so steeped in murmurs of the ocean that its natural dreaminess seems deepened thereby. I cannot find that any barons of the old time or that any world-shaking people have lived there, or that any events which startle a nation ever happened on that ground, but the tranquil charm that fills the air repays for the absence of historic fame.

There is seldom much stir in Norbreck, except such as the elements make. The inhabitants would think the place busy with a dozen people upon its grass-grown road at once, whatever the season might be. It is true that on a fine day in summer I have now and then seen a little life just at the entrance of the hamlet. There stands a pretty cottage, of one storey, consisting of six cosy rooms, that run lengthwise, its white walls adorned with rose-trees and fruit-trees, and its windows bordered with green trellis-work. Two trim grass-plots, with narrow beds of flowers, and neat walks, mosaically-paved with blue and white pebbles from the sea, fill up the front garden, which a low white wall and a little green gate enclose from the road. In

141

front of this cottage I have sometimes seen a troop of rosy children playing round a pale girl, who was hopelessly infirm, and, perhaps on that account, the darling of the whole household. I have seen her rocking in the sun, and with patient melancholy watching their gambols, whilst they strove to please her with all kinds of little artless attentions. Poor Lucy! Sometimes after swaying to and fro thoughtfully in her chair, she would stop and ask questions that sent her father out of the room to wipe his eyes. "Papa, are people lame in heaven?" "Papa, are angels poorly sometimes, like we are here?".....It is one of those beautiful compensations that mingle with the mishaps of life, that such a calamity has often the sweet effect of keeping kind hearts continually kind. The poor Lancashire widow, when asked why she seemed to fret more for the loss of her helpless lad than for any of her other children, said she couldn't tell, except "it were becose hoo'd had to nurse him moor nor o' tother put together." Surely,

There is a soul of good in all things evil.

About this pretty cottage, where Lucy lived, is the busiest part of the hamlet in summer time. There may chance to be two or three visitors sauntering in the sunshine; or, perhaps, old Thomas Smith, better known as "Owd England", the sea-beaten patriarch of Norbreck, may paddle across the road to look after his cattle, or, staff in hand, may be going down to "low watter" a-shrimping, with his thin hair playing in the breeze. Perhaps Lizzy, the milkmaid, may run from the house to the shippon, with her skirt tucked up, and the neb of an old bonnet pulled down to shade her eyes; or Tom, the cow-lad, may be leaning against a sunny wall, whistling, and mending his whip, and wondering how long it wants to dinner-time. There may be a fine cat dozing on the garden wall or gliding steathily towards the outhouses. These are common features of life there. For the rest, the sounds heard are mostly the cackle of poultry, the clatter of milk-cans, the occasional bark of a dog, the distant lowing of kine, a snatch of country song floating from the fields, the wild birds'

Tipsy routs of lyric joy,

and that all-embracing murmur of the surge which fills one's ears wherever we go. In Norbreck everything smacks of the sea. On the grassy border of the road, about the middle of the hamlet, there is generally a pile of wreck waiting the periodical sale which takes place all along the coast. I have sometimes looked at this pile, and thought that perhaps to this or that spar some seaman might have clung with desperate energy among the hungry waters, until he sank, overpowered, into his uncrowded grave. The walls of gardens and farmyards are mostly built of cobbles from the beach, sometimes fantastically laid in patterns of different hues. The garden beds are edged with shells, and the walks laid with blue and white pebbles. Here and there are rockeries of curiously-shaped stones from the shore. Every house has its little store of marine rarities, which meet the eye on cornices and shelves wherever we turn. Now and then we meet with a dead sea-mew on the road, and noisy flocks of gulls make fitful excursions landward, particularly in ploughing time when they crowd after the plough to pick slugs and worms out of the new furrows.

With a single exception, all the half-dozen dwellings in Norbreck are on one side of the road, with their backs to the north. On the one side there are gardens, and a few whitewashed outhouses, with weather-beaten walls. The main body of the hamlet consists of a great irregular range of buildings, formerly the residence of a wealthy family. This pile is now divided into several dwellings, in some of which are snug retreats for such as prefer the seclusion of this sea-nest to the bustle of a crowded watering-place. A little enclosed lawn, belonging to the endmost of the group, and then a broad field, divides this main cluster from the only other habitation. The latter seems to stand off a little, as if it had more pretensions to gentility than the rest. It is a picturesque house, of different heights, built at different times. At the landward end, a spacious yard, with great wooden doors close to the road, contains the out-buildings, with an old-fashioned weather vane on the top of them. The lowermost part of the dwelling is a combination of neat cottages of one storey. The highest part is a substantial brick edifice of two stories, with attics. This portion has great bow windows, which sweep the sea view, from the coast of Wales, round by the Isle of Man, to the mountains of Cumberland. In summer, the white walls of the cottage part are covered with roses and creeping plants, and there is an air of order and tasteful rusticity about the whole, even to the neat cobble pavement which borders the way-side. On the top of the porch a stately peacock sometimes struts, like a feathered showman, whilst his mate paces to and fro, cackling, on the field wall immediately opposite. There are probably a few poultry pecking about the front; and, if it happens to be a sunny day, a fine old English bear-hound, of the Lyme breed, called Lion, and not much unlike his namesake in *the main, they may be seen stretched in a sphinx-like posture in the middle of the road, as if the whole Fylde belonged to him, by right of entail, and slowly moving his head with majestic gaze, as if turning over in his mind whether or not it would be polite to take a piece out of the passing traveller for presuming to walk that way. Perhaps in the southward fields a few kine are grazing and whisking their tails in the sunshine, or galloping from gap to gap under the influence of the gad-fly's spur; and it may happen that some wanderer from Blackpool can be seen on the cliffs, with his garments flapping in the breeze. Except these, and the rolling surge below, all is still at this end of the hamlet, unless the jovial face of the owner appears above the wall that encloses his outbuildings, wishing the passer-by "the fortune of the day." Norbreck, as a whole, is no way painfully genteel in appearance, but it is sweet and serene, and its cluster of houses seems to know how to be comfortable, without caring much for display. Dirt and destitution are unknown there,—in fact, I was told that this applies generally to all the scattered population of that quiet Fylde country. Though there are many people there whose means of existence are almost as simple as those of the wild bird and the field-mouse, yet squalor and starvation are strangers amongst them. If any mischance happens to any of these Fylde folk, everybody knows everybody else, and, some how, they stick to one another like Paddy's shrimps—if you take up one you take up twenty. The road, which comes up thither from many a mile of playful meandering through the green country, as soon as it quits the last house immediately dives through the cliffs, with a sudden impulse, as if it had been reading "Robinson Crusoe", and had been drawn all that long way solely by its love for the ocean. The sea-beach at this spot is a fine sight at any time; but in a clear sunset the scene is too grand to be touched by any imperfect words. Somebody has very well called this part of the coast "the region of glorious sunsets". When the waters retire, they leave a noble solitude, where a man may wander a mile or two north or south upon a floor of sand finer than any marble, "and yet no fotting seen" except his own; and hear no sounds that mingle with the mysterious murmurs of the sea but the cry of the sailing gull, the piping of a flock of silver-winged tern, or the scream of the wild sea-mew. Even in summer there are but few stragglers to disturb those endless forms of beauty which the moody waves, at every ebb, leave printed all over that grand expanse, in patterns ever new.*

Such is little Norbreck, as I have seen it in the glory of the year. In winter, when the year's whitewash upon its houses is getting a little weather-worn, it looks rather moulty and ragged to the eye; and it is more lonely and wild, simply because Nature itself is so then,—and Norbreck and Nature are not very distant relations.

It was a bonny day on the 5th of March, 1860, when I visited Norbreck, just before those tides came on which had been foretold as higher than any for a century previous. This announcement brought thousands of people from the interior into Blackpool and other places on that coast. Many came expecting the streets to be invaded by the tide, and a great part of the level Fylde laid under water, with boats plying above the deluged fields, to rescue its inhabitants from the towers of churches and the tops of farmhouses. Knowing as little of these things as inland people generally do, I had something of the same expectation; but when I came to the coast, and found the people going quietly about their usual business, I thought that, somehow, I must be wrong. It is true that one or two farmers had raised their stacks several feet, and another had sent his "deeds" to Preston, that they might be high and dry till the waters left his land again; and certain old ladies who had been reading the newspapers were a little troubled thereby; but, in the main, these seaside folk did not seem afraid of the tide.

During the two days when the sea was to reach its height, Blackpool was as gay, and the weather almost as fine, as if it had been the month of June instead of "March,—mony weathers," as Fylde folk call it. The promenade was lively with curious inlanders, who had left their looms at this unusual season to see the wonders of the great deep. But when it came to pass that, because there was no wind to help in the water, the tide rose but little higher than common, many people murmured thereat, and the town emptied as quickly as it had filled. Not finding a deluge, they hastened landward again, with a painful impression that the whole thing was a hoax. The sky was blue, the wind was still, and the sun was shining clearly; but this was not what they had come forth to see.

(Edwin Waugh Lancashire Sketches 1881)

★   ★   ★   ★   ★

A practical-minded visitor thus celebrates its claim to consideration:-

Of all the gay places of public resort,
At Chatham or Scarbro', at Bath or at Court,
There's none like sweet Blackpool, of which I can boast,
So charming the sands, so healthful the coast; —
Rheumatics, scorbutics, and scrofulous kind,
Hysterics and vapours, disorders of mind,
By drinking and bathing you're made quite anew,
As thousands have proved, and know to be true.
But strange! I relate what has happened of late—
'Tis true! though I heard on't but now tete-a-tete,
Still, lest you mistake me, I'll fully explain—
Young Cupid, 'tis said, lies hid in yon main,
And philters each wave that rolls on the shore,
A draught daily drank by the rich and the poor.
The ladies, well pleas'd with a potion so sweet,
Come here in whole groups their fond lovers to meet;
And gentlemen, too, who are friends to the fair,
Come under pretence to enjoy the fresh air.

(An anonymous poem from DODWELL. Lancashire: Pocket Companion 1895)

★　　★　　★　　★

Blackpool! How differently that talismatic name affects one as the years get on. What an almost incredible difference is experienced between the first time of going, in the early flush of youth, and the same journey in maturer years. Though people may tell us that it is ourselves and not Blackpool that has changed, yet we cling a little to the consoling idea that Blackpool is not what it used to be. But whatever may be said to the contrary, if anyone will have the temerity to venture on an early Whit Monday trip thither ocular demonstration may be had that the youth of today enjoys the outing quite as boisterously and keenly as the youth of twenty-five years ago did. And there is no doubt that for certain temperaments and certain purposes, Blackpool, with all its monotony, is a very enjoyable place; and being made by the railway companies so very easy of access great numbers of people take advantage of the opportunities to inhale its salubrious breezes ....

I always think that a good tea is as enjoyable as anything in Blackpool, provided you can watch the promenaders at the time you are having it, and I am not quite sure that a good meal is not the most enjoyable thing whether you can watch the promenaders or not.

After tea we must, of course, have a stroll round and see the sights, which said sights are indelibly printed on my mind; not by virtue of this visit, but on account of previous experiences.

There was the ever present diminutive specimen of humanity with the useless nether limbs and expressionless eyes, sitting on his chair of locomotion, with his small donations thankfully received can prominently before him as usual. There was the stall with the prawns, which the vendor will persist in calling shrimps. And there was, as there always is, the oyster stall next to him, the owner of which told me that, if I would try a few they would 'make my blooming neck swell.' As I didn't want to have a swelled neck, I didn't have any. Then a little farther on we came to a blind man with a voice like a sea trumpet, accompanying himself on a harmonium, and singing a song about a sailor who was swallowed by a whale, and who then put his hand out and seized the whale by the tail and turned himself inside out. So we went on for fear there might be more of it.

We hadn't proceeded far, in fact we'd hardly proceeded at all, when we came upon another blind man and a girl, with a harmonium, singing in a very mild treble one of Moody and Sankey's hymns, in which a few individuals in the small audience that had collected round them were making spasmodic attempts to join. As this wasn't exactly what we had come to see, and there being a crowd about forty yards further on we went to see what it was. Here was a girl of about thirteen, with a very existence-out-of-doors look on her face, singing with another blind man who played another harmonium. They were singing 'The sweet by and bye,' and oh, the mouth of that blind man when he came to the 'by and bye'! It may be very bad taste to dwell on the subject, but that face I am afraid will ever haunt me. I couldn't describe it, nor would I try, but it reminded me of some small stone faces that I used, when a boy, to see ornamenting the singers' gallery surrounding the Blackburn Parish Church organ. A little further on was another blind man, a girl and a harmonium, and further on it was repeated, until we got to the North Pier. There seems to me to be a superabundance of blind man and harmonium; in fact, I consider it to be the prevailing feature at Blackpool.

Well, we promenaded, and we sometimes stopped to listen to the groups of singers. We enjoyed the breeze and admired the electric light which I consider has a very striking resemblance to bright moonlight, but is less soft and more weird. In this manner, as thousands before us have done, we idled the time away till within a few minutes of the hour for returning, and then we proceeded to the Central Station.

(*Sigil* (George Jones) 1888)

★   ★   ★   ★   ★

It's a question whether Blackpool ever held so mony visitors i' one week as it did this last Whit-week, an' as aw dar say it'll be referred to i' yers to come as th' biggest week ever known. Everything wer i' its favor. Th' sun wer on full time an' hee pressure every day, an' th'
'Moon taking hold of the reins of night,
Drove steadily on in her chariot of light'
which rendered neet lovely. Th' mornin' tide flowed gently in beawt th' semblance of a ripple on the surface, which gan th' boatmen a chance o' reapin' a little—an' much needed—harvest, and then gracefully retired in favor of an afternoon's innings for th' donkey drivers. Punch and Judy skriked an' knocked thersels into a good business, an' th' minstrels did a roerin' trade. Th' wax-works had getten a 'correct likeness o' th' latest murderer' (afore one had bin seen), an' as th' mon at th' dur sed, Kings an' queens of o' sizes, sexes, an' ages,' which drew in hosts of the curious. Aw th' piers wer crammed, an' ther're steamer sailins to different places fro' each. Aw never saw sich a thing i' mi life, th' streets wer as thrung at seven o'clock i' th' morning as Market Street, Manchester, is at one o'clock of a Setterday. Bands o' music wer playing an' on th' South Pier ther're a lot o' young folk gooin' through a set o' quadrilles. Neaw just fancy that! Aw've known o' parties startin at th' o'er neet an' dancin till welly that time i' th' morning, but this is fust time aw ever saw or knew 'em to start so early i' th' mornin', an' that i' th' oppen too. Passin' on up th' North Shore at th' same time aw saw billiards bein plyed through th' window of a hotel known as th' Palatine. Th' rulin' passion—yoa see—strung at any time an' any wheer. Vehicles wi' horses an' beawt horses were movin' cargoes o' livin' freight abeawt, an' th' artists' studios cudn't find even stonding room for their

148

subjects. It wer a pleasure to me watchin' folk enjoy thersels, each after their kind—though sum on 'em wer a bit rough, an' own't to ha' been let loose.

(Rambles and recollections of 'R' Dick by Robert Dottie
1898)

★ ★ ★ ★ ★

A great attraction to Blackpool is its marine promenade with carriage drive, extending in an unbroken length for three miles along the water's edge. The sea washes at high water the embankment of the promenade, often coming into the streets, and at low water recedes about a quarter of a mile, leaving sands which, for their golden colour, extent, dryness, and hardness, are not excelled in England. The bathing is excellent, the water becoming deep very gradually and there are numerous machines at various points. There are three splendid piers, all iron-built, named the North, Central and Victoria (At South-shore) respectively. The North Pier, an elegant structure, enjoys the largest share of patronage—indeed such was the crowding upon the pier that the directors expended £20,000 in widening and extending the pier-head, upon which have been erected shops, and a handsome pavilion, wherein are held excellent concerts; lectures, swimming, and other entertainments are also given, and, when fine, open-air concerts are given by an efficient orchestra. The Victoria pier caters for the public in a similar manner to the North Pier, by means of a good orchestra and variety entertainments. At each pier there is an extension or jetty for the large steamer traffic.

In the Winter Gardens and at Palace Gardens are two good theatres, besides other entertainments of a like character. At Palace Gardens, agricultural and horti-cultural shows, athletic sports dancing, displays of fire-works, etc., take place. A large monkey house and aviary have been built; and seals, otters, and aquatic birds are kept. Amusements are also provided each season in the pavilion. A large tower, after the model of the famous one in Paris, has been built and is now open, and the old aquarium and menagerie have been incorporated with it. The tower is so large that there is room on the top for over 1,000 people to promenade at one time. The top is reached by a series of lifts. The basement has been utilised as an aquatic and variety circus. The Winter Gardens are on a large scale in a central position. In the theatre, which is equal to any in the provinces,

*concerts and other performances are given during the
season, and during the remainder of the year operas,
dramas, etc., are performed.....*

*The prices for lodgings and board at the hotels, of which
there are large numbers, range from 10s. 6d. upwards per
day, and private sitting rooms from 30s. per week. The
prices of lodgings in private houses vary from 7s. to 12s.
per week for a bedroom, and from 15s. to 40s. for sitting
rooms, though even lower prices are asked in some of the
back streets.*

(From *Seaside Watering Places* 1898)

★   ★   ★   ★   ★

*It worn't long befoor they faund thersens on th' edge of a
craad listenin' to a young man wearin' a topper an'
white waistcoit, an' howdin' up a small bottle in his hand.*

*'Ladies and gentlemen', he began, 'I have in this bottle a
solution which I guarantee—guarantee, bear in mind—will
enable you to remove corns absolutely without pain, no
matter what their size, whether hard or soft, of long or
short standing. This solution is the product of many years'
experimental research. I have not come to the Blackpool
sands with the object of making money, for the reputation
of the liquid is already too well established in other parts
of the country to place me under that necessity. No, I am
here in the interest of humanity. I asked myself this
question: 'Why should this boon be limited to one part of
the country alone, when there are thousands of people
scattered all over the universe who are at this very
moment enduring martyrdom from the presence of
corns on their toes?' Yes, ladies and gentlemen, I felt that I
had a duty to discharge to suffering humanity, and that
explains why I am here—here in Blackpool, with its
palaces of pleasure, its noble piers, its beautiful sands, its
marvellous promenade, its invigorating air and its
glorious and boundless expanse of ocean! But what are
these to you if every step you take brings forth a groan?
Why endure this perpetual torment when relief is near
at hand? I know you are naturally suspicious of me,
because there are so many quacks around seeking
with smooth tongues and plausible tales to beguile you
out of your hard earned money. I beg of you not to
associate me with them; in order to convince you that
this remedy is genuine, I invite anyone present who is
afflicted with corns to kindly step forward and allow me to
test it.'*

For a minnit or two ther' wor nooa response, but at last a chap i'th'front stepped forrard, sat daan on a low chair, pulled off his booits an' stockin's, an' browt into view a pair o' feet 'at hadn't been acquainted wi' sooap an' watter for an age. Bob also nooaticed 'at some of 'em in'th'inner circle held the'r nooases sky'ards.

'Now, then, ladies and gentlemen, let me call your attention to the method of operating. How long have you been troubled with this corn?' axed th'operator, at th' same time pressin' his thumb on it.

'Howd on, theer!' th' patient yelled out, 'aw've hed it monny a year.'

'Have you never tried to get rid of it?,

'Yes, aw've tried o'sooarts. Aw've spent monny a peaund on't, off an' on.'

'You hear what the gentleman says. He has tried all kinds of so-called corn removers without any effect. Now to show you that mine is no sham, but the genuine article I claim it to be, I intend to remove this corn within the space of one minute. First of all you pour two drops of the solution on the top of the corn, and rub it gently in, then get a lance or sharp penknife, carefully cut round the cap, and there you are!' howdin' up th' corn between his fingers.

He then seeazed howd o'th'patient's tooa, twirled it raand, an' axed him if he felt onny pain.

'Now, that's o' reet, lad. Let's hev a bottle', he replied.

'Ladies and gentlemen', said th'operator, turnin' ageean to th' craad, 'I have given you a practical illustration of the efficacy of this wonderful liquid. If any of you care to purchase, the price is one shilling; at my private address it will be half-a-crown. It is worth at least a guinea a bottle, and on every one sold at a shilling I lose money. Now who says a bottle?'

Dozens of hands wor stretched aat in a twinklin', Bob's amang 'em. As sooin as he gat a bottle, he set off wi' his wife to see what wor takkin' place i' th' next group, abaat a dozen yards off.

Here ther wor a tent rigged up, wi' theeas words painted on th' canvas: Professor Bumpem, the world-renowned palmist and phrenologist. Th' purfessor wor runnin' his hands ovver a big fat woman's noddlebox, talkin' away all th' time.

'This lady', he wor sayin', 'is a very remarkable character. Whatever sphere she had been born in, she would have filled it well. Willpower and individuality are clearly marked. Had the lady happened to belong to the *opposite sex, she would undoubtedly have made an excellent general, for the commanding faculty is strongly developed.'*

'It's true, maister', said a little shrunken chap nearby, who evidently had a life interest i' th' party under examination.

'Cum on, aw'm tired o' this humbug. Let's have a look at them niggers ovver theer', said Bob.

Ther' wor a big audience raand theeas imitations, who wor carryin' on a dialogue summat after this style:

'I say, Joey?'

'Waal?'

'Can you tell me why Blackpool is an aristocratic place?' After scratchin' his head th' other chap says he'll give up.

'Because there are never less than three piers upon its shore.'

(From *Bob Blunt's Trip to Blackpool* by Tom Platts 1915)

★ ★ ★ ★ ★

Goin' to Blackpool neaw for a day means hevvin a bathe, sixpennorth o' sailin, a ride in a carridge, or else on a donkey an varra often geddin' drunk, an aw towd Mary Ann as we'd try to do o'th lot on em only th' last; an hoo sed ther wor a good reason for thad as hoo dudn't think as ther wer enough o' weet i' th' teawn to mek mo drunk, an hoo give o th' sawt wayter in. Well, we went daewn on to th' sands among some moor donkeys, boath two leg'd uns an four leg'd uns—one o'th top o' th' other, some on em wor. Ther wer a lot o' them wood boxes upo' wheels, wi' step lathers danglin' at back, as they co'd bathin' vans, as they took into th' sea wi' a hoss. Eawr Mary Ann co'd um weshin' machines, an aw believe hoo wer reight, for they'n nasty lots in em sometimes—ids no wonder at sea bein' a bad colour.

(From:-A Day at Blackpool by John Almond)

"(Blackpool) is pleasure without pretentiousness, refreshment within the reach of those who need it most, fun without those unnecessary frills which add so little to enjoyment and so much to expense. In a word, Blackpool is the place where you get more for your money than anywhere else on earth."

(James Laver 'Beside the Seaside' (Bodley Head 1934)

GOOD OWD BLACKPOOL!
by William Baron (Bill o' Jack's) 1910

When th' "Wakes" brings its welcome holiday,
An' labour for th' time gives way to play;
Eawr Lankisher toilers, uv every class,
Pack up for th' "briny," to melt ther brass.
Ther's lots o' places areawnd eawr coast,
O' which we may truly an' justly boast,
*But th' **one** 'at appeals to th' masses most*
    Is bracin', breezy Blackpool!

Wi' its four-mile "prom," an' its matchless sea,
It fears no rivals, wheere'er they be;
On its endless stretches o' gowden sands
Yo may listen to th' pierrots, an' minstrel bands.
Ther's amusements i' plenty for young an' owd,
Fun to suit th' timid, an' fun for th' bowd,
While th' lasses con hev ther fortin's towd
    Bi th' gipsies deawn at Blackpool.

Should th' fine weather change to a storm, or shower,
Ther's th' Winter Gardens, an' th' Palace, an' th' Tower,
In ony o' these yo may spend a day,
An' a "tanner's" o 'at yo hev to pay.
If a strange sensation yo want to feel,
Gooa in for a journey reawnd th' Big Wheel,
An' yor satisfaction yo'll not conceal
    At th' view yo get o' Blackpool.

Its joys, an' its ozone-laden air,
Mek it a place beyond compare;
It ston's unequalled, 'twixt earth an' skies,
As a pleasure-seeker's paradise.
Some 'mid quateness are best content,
Others luv tourin' on th' Continent,
But for health an' pleasure, supremely blent,
    Ther's nowt like good owd Blackpool!

William Baron (1865-1927) wrote this poem for his magazine, *Bill o'Jack's Lancashire Monthly* in 1910. Although he lived most of his life in Blackburn and Rochdale he had a love of Blackpool, and his poem *A Peep at Mi Birthplace* is to be found in his book *Echoes From The Loom* (1903). The family left Blackpool when William was five years old.

★ ★ ★ ★ ★

GOOD ENOUGH FOR ME by J.J. Roberts (c.1925)

Dear Blackpool with its mighty sea
Is plenty good enough for me.
If I can't travel to the Rhine
On no account will I repine,
So long as Lancashire can boast
Of such a sea and such a coast.

The Danube may be very nice;
The Poles may beckon with their ice;
The mighty Tower of Paris may
Be just the place to spend a day;
But Blackpool sands and Blackpool sea
Are plenty good enough for me.